RED EARTH

Tales of the Mi'kmaq
With an introduction to the customs and beliefs of the Mi'kmaq

by Marion Robertson

NIMBUS PUBLISHING LTD

Nimbus Publishing Limited
PO Box 9166, Halifax, NS B3K 5M8
(902) 455-4286

Printed and bound in Canada

Design: Mauve Pagé
Illustrations are from the George Creed tracings of petroglyphs from Lake Kedjimkoojik, Queens County, N.S., now in the Nova Scotia Museum

Library and Archives Canada Cataloguing in Publication

Robertson, Marion, 1910-1998
Red earth : tales of the Micmacs / Marion Robertson.
First ed. published: Halifax : Nova Scotia Museum, c1969.
Includes bibliographical references.
ISBN 1-55109-575-0

1. Micmac Indians—Folklore. 2. Legend—Maritime Provinces. I. Title.

E99.M6R66 2006   398.2089'97343   C2006-901966-5

We acknowledge the financial support of the Government of Canada through the Book Publishing Industry Development Program (BPIDP) and the Canada Council, and of the Province of Nova Scotia through the Department of Tourism, Culture and Heritage for our publishing activities.

CONTENTS

1   **Customs and Beliefs of the Mi'kmaq**

Tales and Traditions of the Mi'kmaq

Tales of Niscaminou—the Very Great
21   How Niscaminou made the Mi'kmaq
22   Niscaminou and the Squirrels of the Blue Mountains

Tales of the Stars and the Moon
24   The Sisters Who Married Stars
29   Mooin and the Seven Hunters
32   Moon Chief

Tales of the Origin of Things
34   How the Loon Became a Sea Bird
35   How the Bullfrog Got His Hunched Back
36   Indian Corn and Tobacco
37   The Storm-maker

Tales of the Little People
40   The Little People
41   The Three Brothers and the Little People
43   The Indian Who Became a Megumoowesoo
46   The Invisible Hunter
49   How Summer was Brought Back to the Land of the Mi'kmaq

Tales of the Great Glooscap
51   How Niscaminou Made Glooscap
52   Glooscap and His Twin Brother Malsum
53   Glooscap and Mikchikch
55   The Call of the Loon
56   The First Cedar Tree
58   Glooscap's Footprints
58   The Bird Islands
60   How Glooscap Left the Mi'kmaq

CONTENTS (CONTINUED)

Tales and Historical Traditions

64   The Great Chief Uglimoo

67   Wokun

68   Magua of Refugee Cove

70   Memajoookun

73   **Mi'kmaq Informants**

75   **Notes**

87   **Bibliography**

For Maria Leach

Profile of Indian Head

CUSTOMS AND BELIEFS OF THE MI'KMAQ

"Old times," said old Mali, "this was all Indian land. Good land for Indian – hunt, fish. Now no more. White man come; Indian go. Too bad Indian go."

Old Mali stood among her baskets remembering old times, her hands as brown as the hands of the old Indians she longed for. Her people were the Mi'kmaq – an Algonquian tribe of Indians of Eastern Woodland culture, and one of the six Wabanaki tribes which include the Maliseet, the Passamaquoddy, the Penobscot, the Wowenoch, and the Abenaki Indians. In the old times her people lived in all of Nova Scotia, in Prince Edward Island, along the west coast of Newfoundland, in New Brunswick to the east bank of the St. John River, and along the southern and eastern shores of the Gaspé Peninsula. Living as they did close to the sea, they were among the first Indians to know the white man when he came in his great white-winged ships into the bays and inlets of the North Atlantic. This book is the story of old Mali's people, the old Mi'kmaq, as they were when the first white men found them, and some of the tales which they told around their campfires.

Hunting

In the old days the Mi'kmaq thought of their land as a mighty giant with one foot at "land's end" at Yarmouth, the other at Gaspé, and his head, the island of Cape Breton. This was the land they knew as Megumaagee, a word which perhaps meant "red earth country" from *megakumegek*, "red ground" "red earth" and the suffix "age" meaning "country". That all the Indians might have a good place to hunt and to fish, they divided their land into districts, each with a chief, whose duty it was to assign to each hunter or family the hunting territories within his district. This he did every spring and fall in the assembly of the elders. No Indian was permitted to overstep the bounds of his land, and each killed only what was needed, for the existence of his family depended upon the preservation of the fish and game within his allotted grounds.

The Mi'kmaq did most of their hunting in the winter in the shelter of the forest, and fished in the summer. They knew many ways of hunting and fishing, varying their methods with the seasons and the habits of the animals and fish. Salmon and trout were speared at night by torch light in the pools where they rested after jumping the water falls. Sturgeon and bass were taken with harpoons and lances from the side of a canoe as they circled into the rim of light cast by burning torches. To catch eels and other small fish a bag net was placed in the opening of a wooden fence built across a river where it was narrowest and had the least water. In the summer bears were killed wherever they were found. In the winter, during hibernation, the Mi'kmaq looked at large hollow trees to see if there was any sign of breath coming as a vapour from within. If they saw signs of a bear they mounted the tree and killed it with their spears and drew it out. Beavers were hunted with bows and arrows in the woods or on the lakes and ponds by canoe, or their dams were broken open and they were taken with spears or arrows as they fled from their houses, or they were captured in traps baited with a strip of aspen. To find moose the Indians looked for twigs of a year's growth where they had browsed, and from the taste of the broken tip they knew how recently the moose had passed that way. With great patience they sought to take them in ambush or stalked them with dogs through the deep snow until they fell fatigued and were easily killed. To entice their prey within range of their arrows the Mi'kmaq had a call for every animal: for a deer, a snort to imitate the stag; for the otter, a whistle; for the beaver, a hiss.

Moose was always the favourite food of the Mi'kmaq and when one was killed the hunter slit open the skin and took the heart, kidneys, tongue, entrails, and fat and hurried to his wigwam. On these his family and friends feasted while the women and girls went off dancing and singing to bring in the moose, for never did an Indian hunter bring home the meat he had killed. That was the work of the women who flayed and dressed the moose, cut up the meat and carried it to the village. If there had been a famine, now there was plenty, for the meat belonged not to the one who had killed it or to his family alone, but to all the Indians, and he who had killed it had least of all for he served the others.

Food

Early in the spring the Mi'kmaq left the shelter of the forest for their summer camping grounds along the shores. It was the happy time of the year for the

Fishing from canoes

Mi'kmaq, and with meat, fish, fowl, and fresh eggs in abundance they held their feast of thankfulness for food. Although there were many kinds of food the Mi'kmaq always had only one kind of meat or fish at their feasts, accompanied on special occasions by the drinking of oil and melted grease. With an abundance of food around them they remembered the hungry days of winter and put aside a portion for the moons of snow and ice, but never did they put aside enough to tide them over the lean days when hunting was poor. For winter use, meat, fowl, and fish, lobsters, and other shell fish were smoked and sun-dried; berries were boiled, shaped into cakes and dried in the sun to be used in soup. Egg yolks were boiled hard, dried and powdered for broth; bones were broken and boiled for the marrow; fat and oil were stored in seal bladders. Nuts and wild beach peas were gathered and the roots of *segubun* (the wild Indian potato, which an old Mi'kmaq remembered as yellow and sweet and much like the southern sweet potato). In times of famine when the food they had prepared for winter was gone, and the hunters killed no game, the Indians chewed the inner rind of birch and poplar, boiled the parings of skins, and ate their old moccasins.

In the old days, according to Marc Lescarbot, the Mi'kmaq did a little gardening which they soon put aside when they could trade furs with the French for bread and dried peas and beans. An interesting early Portugese place-name on the south shore of Nova Scotia, Ribera des Jardins, now known as the Jordan River, is believed to have been given for old Mi'kmaq gardens. On Long Island in the Roseway River, a few miles west of the Jordan River, the Mi'kmaq had small plots of land under cultivation when the first white settlers were given grants of land on the island, and they and their chief Joseph Luxy pleaded that the land which they had tilled should not be given to others.

But the Mi'kmaq, even in the old days, never did enough gardening to hold them long in one place, and when fish and game became scarce in one location they moved to another, sometimes many miles away. It was the work of the women to carry all they possessed, including the poles and the bark of the wigwam, to the new campsite, as it was womens' work to erect the wigwam and to make it comfortable for all who lived within its bark walls.

The Wigwam

To make a wigwam, poles were stuck into the earth in a circle, drawn together in a peak, and held in place by a stout hoop tied to the inside of the poles about six feet above the ground. Layers of birch bark sewed together with fir roots were laid horizontally as tiles over the outside of the poles, or the poles were covered with skins or with mats of reeds. Twigs of fir to the depth of four fingers covered the floor except for the center of the wigwam where the fire was made.

The Mi'kmaq also built rectangular wigwams of upright posts or of horizontal logs with a bark superstructure. These were sometimes very large with three or four fireplaces and were lived in by several families. Some of their villages were enclosed with a thick wall of trees tied securely one against the other.

Inside the wigwam the mistress sat next to the door and to the right of the fire; the master sat beside her and nearer to the back of the wigwam. Opposite the master and the mistress were the old people if there were any in the wigwam; if not, then the young people. Each sat as custom decreed: the men, cross-legged; the women with their legs twisted to one side, one foot above the other; little children with their feet straight before them.

The back of the wigwam was reserved for honoured guests. To a friend the master called out joyfully, "Come up to the back of the wigwam, my friend." To the unwelcome visitor the greeting was a sharp, "What is your wish?" One who came in the day stepped inside the wigwam and greeted the occupants with a hearty *"Kwa,"* or, "Ho, ho, ho." At night the greeting was said outside the doorway, and the master of the wigwam inquired, "Who are you?" If invited to sit in the place of honour the master filled a pipe with tobacco, lit it, drew a long draught of smoke from the bowl and passed it to the honoured guest. If there were others it was passed on until all had drawn smoke from the pipe of welcome. The mistress of the wigwam stirred the fire, the pot bubbled and boiled, meat was served on a platter of birch bark, and in the flickering light of their campfire they remembered their long tales of adventure and the great events in their land.

Clothing

The Indians made their clothes of skins, and both men and women had the same kind of garments. In the summer they wore a breechcloth of soft skin attached to a leather belt. In the winter they drew a cloak around their shoulders tied with a leather thong, and had separate sleeves which they tied together behind, or they wore coats, with or without sleeves. When the men went hunting they wore long leggings tied to their belts, and moccasins on their feet. Usually the Indians went bareheaded, but they had a small cap which covered the crown of the head and a peaked or pointed one something like a hood which came down around the neck. For festive occasions, and when they marched off to war, the men had a crown of moose or stag hair painted red and fastened to a band of leather three fingers wide, or they wore one made from the two wings of a bird. For festive occasions the Mi'kmaq also had robes like a blanket made of skins or the plumage of the wild goose. As their other dress-up garments, which were fringed and painted in lace-like patterns, the Mi'kmaq decorated their robes with rows of embroidery and with the figures of birds and animals. Robes were worn by the men across their shoulders, tied with a cord beneath the chin and allowed to fall open; women made an opening in theirs for the head to pass through the middle of the robe, wrapped it around them and held the folds with a girdle.

Both boys and girls let their hair grow full length: the boys with theirs tied with a cord in two tufts, one each side; the girls with theirs tied behind. Men and women had their hair cut below the ears as a symbol of marriage; otherwise they let it fall to their shoulders and generally wore it loose, except when the men trussed theirs up to the crown of the head and let it fall behind. Sometimes they braided their hair and bound into the tresses strings of beadwork and wampum, or ornaments made of coloured quills woven into a warp of soft moose skin. The Mi'kmaq greased their hair to make it shine, and when they painted their faces they painted their hair the same colour.

Ornaments

The endless toil for food and shelter, clothes and warmth did not strangle the Indians' longing to express in paint, wood, stone, and bone their desire for beauty. In the dim light of campfires in the long winter nights, and in the warm days of summer when the needs of life were not so pressing, they took into their calloused hands pieces of stone or wood or a bit of bone and, feeling the spirit of the stone or the wood or the bone, they carved with wonder and delight a bird, a beast, or a man. That the work of their hands may at times seem crude to us of a different culture is neither here nor there; that they strove to express the inner spirit of joy in beauty is all that matters.

Both the free flowing figure and the hardened angular lines of the geometric intrigued the Mi'kmaq. Series of triangles, conventional designs of intricate lines and angles, lace-like patterns of great delicacy, and the lovely double curve design famous among the Algonquians were employed to good advantage. Animals, birds, and other designs were embroidered in thread or with quills or were sketched and painted on their clothing, cradleboards, wigwams, and canoes, and ornaments were made of quills dyed red, white, and black. Beads were made from shells and from wood and from the cross section of the leg and

Peaked headdress

the wing bones of birds. Bear and lynx teeth, the incisors of the moose, the toe bones of bears, and the skulls of birds were perforated and worn as amulets.

Paint for their clothing, wigwams, and canoes was made by the Mi'kmaq from red and yellow ochre, from pot black, from charcoal, and from powdered shells mixed with grease. A brilliant red dye was made from bedstraw; a bright yellow came from gold thread. Paint was applied to skin and bark with isinglass and the colour made fast by passing over it a piece of hot bone.

Tools and Pottery

All that the Mi'kmaq possessed came from the labour of their hands, and for everything that they made they first had to make a tool: adzes, hammerstones, gouges, flakers, axes, choppers, whetstones and wedges, chisels and knives, scrapers and peelers, awls and needles. These they made from bone, stone, wood, antler, and a few from copper. With them they shaped bows and arrows, harpoons, spears, plummets, clubs and shields; made their bark canoes, clothes, and wigwams; birch buckets and dishes; boxes and root baskets, cups and spoons.

Pottery was the work of the women. They shaped it from a mass of clay, tempered with grit, or built it up in coils or bands, gave each piece a rounded, a conical, or a sharp pointed bottom, and brought the rim up straight with very little flare, and smoothed the edge flat or waved it according to their fancy. Into the wet clay around the upper portion of the pot they etched lines, rows of dots, squares, and triangles, or pressed a twig twisted with a cord, or made impressions with woven porcupine quills and moose hair. If the potter lacked a stick or a knife or a cord-lashed twig to decorate her jug, with infinite delight she marked it with her finger tips.

Canoes

To make a canoe, the Mi'kmaq stripped from the largest birch trees bark the length of the canoe which they wished to make, some of which Nicolas Denys said were three or four and a half fathoms long, and had a depth to a man's armpit when seated, and were, according to Marc Lescarbot, four feet broad at the center, narrowing towards the ends with a high prow to pass easily over the waves. When all was ready the bark was bent and trimmed to the shape of the intended canoe, and two sticks the thickness of a cane were sewn with fir roots along the inner and upper edge of the bark. Crosspieces of beech were inserted in holes in the sticks to hold the bark apart, the crosspieces diminishing in length at each end to fit the shape of the canoe. The inside was lined with cedar laths held in place by the ribs which were also of cedar and which had been bent in a fire to the shape required, and were held tight beneath the rods sewn to the edge of the bark. The seams, sewn with fine fir roots, were smeared with fir gum chewed by the women and applied to the seams with fire. Paddles were cut from beech, the blade about six inches wide and the length of a man's arm, the handle a little longer than the blade. There were structural differences in the canoes made by the different tribes known by the Mi'kmaq which enabled them to quickly identify an approaching canoe. The Maliseets and the Indians of Passamaquoddy and Penobscot had an even gunwale; the Beothuk, as did the Mi'kmaq, had an elevated gunwale center, but they had a distinctive pointed bottom that differed from the Mi'kmaq, which cut the water, rolling it back from the bow. A sail of bark or one made from the skin of a young moose was used on fine days, and if the wind was favourable they went "as fast as a stone could be thrown." Sometimes a tree or a bush was used for a sail which gave rise to the saying, "Too much bush for a small canoe."

Birch bark served the Indians in many ways besides for their canoes and wigwams. Buckets of bark tightly sewn with cedar, spruce, or fir roots, made good cooking kettles and could be placed over a fire, the bark burning only to the water's edge. Boxes and dishes of birch bark were etched or were decorated with quills in intricate designs. Besides the things they made of bark, the Mi'kmaq made mats of coloured rushes, and baskets woven of roots and rushes. Weaving was done on a small hand loom with twenty or thirty holes drilled in the bars of wood to hold the strands of yarn. Pack straps, belts, and garters, and fine cords to decorate the edge of caps and clothing were woven from yarn spun from caribou, deer, bear, otter, and rabbit hair, the colour of the strands determining the pattern.

Pipes

The old Mi'kmaq made their pipes of stone or from the bone of a moose, from hard wood or of pottery, or they used a cone of twisted bark, a lobster claw, a small pan fitted with a quill, or a leaf of the pitcher plant. Stems were made from a species of willow known as pipestem wood, or they were made of stone bored with endless patience, and were decorated with porcupine quills. *Tamawa,* or as some of the old Mi'kmaq called it, tamahoe, wild Indian tobacco, was held in great veneration. To pass a pipe of burning tamawa, or tamawa mixed with dry red willow bark when it was known as *nespebakun*, was an offering of peace and good will. To accept the pipe was a bond of friendship; to refuse it was a declaration of hostility.

Warfare

Mi'kmaq warfare was fiendish with no mercy shown to warriors taken in battle, nor to any Indian who helped a prisoner to escape. Wars were fought, not for land, but to avenge an insult or the killing of one of their tribe, or to intimidate another nation. Slain enemies were decapitated or scalped and their bodies flayed to make trophies for the victors. The decision to go to war was made in an assembly of the warriors called by the chiefs. He who was greatest among the chiefs made an oration to stir the warriors, and if they agreed with him they shouted, *"Hou."* If they did not like what he said, others spoke, until all had raised the hatchet. Then they feasted, threw off their clothes, painted their faces and the upper part of their bodies red, and seizing their shields and a club, with bow in hand, a quiver full of arrows, and a knife slung around the neck, they marched off in a clamour of fearful howls. Two methods of warfare were pursued by the Mi'kmaq, the secret attack, and the formal declaration when a belt of wampum was sent to the enemy, or messengers went into their country, struck the earth with their hatchets as a sign of hostility, shot two arrows into their largest village and retreated hastily.

A favourite method of warfare was to hide in the enemy's land and entice the hunters by animal cries into a narrow pass through which they must go to hunt, and to spring upon them from ambush. An Indian would die rather than be a prisoner, and if taken by force starved or killed himself. Returning warriors were always greeted with great rejoicing by the women to whom the prisoners were given to torture or for slaves. A warrior who went alone to seek revenge and brought back the head of an enemy was stripped of his clothes and given an old rag to wear while his friends danced and feasted for eight long days and nights, when they gave him, each one, a present for his valour. The widow of a warrior killed in battle stained her face black and did not marry nor eat meat until her husband's death was avenged.

Feasts

With the spirit of revenge strong in the old Mi'kmaq, there must have been many skirmishes, but their lives were not always grim with warfare and the long struggle to exist, for they loved feasting and dancing, singing, wrestling and games of chance and long races. Even a little food was ample excuse for a feast, and the master of the wigwam went to his neighbours, calling, "Come here to my wigwam for I wish to entertain you." Crying, *"Ho, ho, ho,"* the men of the village flocked to his wigwam carrying their bowls made of birch bark, smoked their host's tobacco and ate the meat he tossed to them or offered on the point of a stick. When they had eaten they shouted to the old men and women, to the children and to the young men who had not as yet slain a moose, to finish the feast outside of the wigwam, and the long speeches began, thanking the giver of the feast. He, they said, was like a mighty tree whose roots gave nourishment to the small shrubs, or he was like a healing herb, or like a mild day in cold winter. Then they remembered his father and his great grandfathers and how they too were mighty hunters and made feasts for their friends. Last of all came the women to thank their host. Dancing and hissing, *"heh, heh, heh,"* to a sharp rhythm beat upon a piece of bark by the oldest among them, they spun on their heels, quivering, one hand lifted high. The old woman ceased her sharp tattoo, they all cried *"Yah!"* and retreated, leaving one to thank their host in the name of all.

Dances and Games

The Mi'kmaq danced with all the gusto of strong bodies made supple with vigorous life. Generally they danced in a circle without moving from one place, struck the earth hard with their feet, and sprang upward in a half leap, swinging their arms, held high and close together, in a threatening motion, their hands clenched. One sang, a man or a woman, and beat upon a tree with a stick, the others hissed, *"Het, het, het."* The song ended, they all shouted, *"Heeee. "*

The women and girls had a special dance in which they alone were the dancers. Looking intently at the earth as if they would draw from it some hidden force by the very strength of their contortions, they drew back, pushed out their arms, their hands, and their bodies, writhed, and hissed through their lips like snakes. This they did over and over again until they were wet with perspiration.

Games of chance, contests, racing, and wrestling were an endless joy to the Mi'kmaq. Their old dice game, *woltesakum, waltes,* is still played with all the vigour of the old days. To play it, six bone dice are tossed in a bowl and brought down with a thud against a cushion or some soft object, the fall of the dice indicating the score. Lescarbot in the early seventeenth century watched the Mi'kmaq play a similar game with painted beans, counting the score by colour, and using quills made of reeds for tally sticks.

Language

Those who have studied Mi'kmaq, which is a dialect of the Algonquian language, have found it flexible and expressive with an abundance of words to communicate ideas. Although the old Mi'kmaq had no written language they could convey a message by fire and smoke signals, by the use of little pieces of wood arranged in different ways and strung together into a necklace, or by the means of pictures drawn on bark. An aid to the Mi'kmaq in their picture-writing were the emblems used by the Indians living in the various divisions of the country. In Miramichi the Indians had the figure of a cross; in Restigouche, a salmon; the Mi'kmaq in the main southwestern division of the Miramichi had a sturgeon; those in the little southwestern division, a beaver; and those in the northwestern section, the figure of a man with a drawn bow and arrow. In the pictography of the Wabanaki the Indians of Passamaquoddy were represented by two men paddling a canoe and following a pollock; the Penobscot Indians by a figure of canoemen using pole and paddle in pursuit of an otter; the Maliseets by two men in a canoe both using poles and chasing a muskrat; the Mi'kmaq by two canoemen with paddles and following a deer.

Birth

Customs shaped the thinking and the lives of the Mi'kmaq from birth until death, giving meaning to their way of life, and confering on them an inner sense of well-being from adhering to the accepted way. At birth babies were dipped in the coldest water that could be found, even in winter, and were made to swallow oil or grease before they were nursed by their mothers. In winter they were wrapped in warm furs and sometimes in the skin of a wild goose; in summer in soft skins, and bound to a cradleboard. Whenever the mother left the wigwam her baby went with her on the cradleboard which hung from a strap across her forehead. On her return, the baby, still bound to the cradleboard, was set straight up against a tree or a rock or against the poles of the wigwam or was hung from the branches of a tree, and was never allowed to lie flat on the ground. There was great rejoicing over the birth of a boy, for the life of the nation depended on good hunters. Feasts were given to celebrate his birth, his first tooth, his first step, and again when he killed his first game. The eldest son was generally named for his father with a diminutive to indicate he was the son. The second son was given any name that pleased his parents; the next, the name of the second, with a suitable syllable to denote he was the third son; or the second and third sons were named for some characteristic of the father, as Hawk for the son of a great hunter.

Courtship and Marriage

When a young man went courting he painted his face red, put on new clothes decorated with beads and paint, and went to the wigwam of the girl's father and asked to enter. If he was favoured he was invited by the father to sit in the place of honour; if there was no greeting he turned away and did not enter the wigwam. If he was accepted he spoke to the girl of his choice and gave her a gift; and if she favoured him as a suitor she gave him a gift of her handwork, and he entered her father's wigwam to hunt and to fish for him for a year to prove himself well able to provide for a wife and family. At the end of the year of betrothal if he was still favoured by the girl and her parents, the oldest men, friends, and parents were invited to a feast provided by the bridegroom; and in the presence of all the young girl was given by her mother to the boy as his wife. Marriages were sometimes arranged by the parents but generally the young people themselves choose each other. Most marriages were happy. Those which were not, the two concerned had only to tell their friends that they no longer shared the same wigwam to be free to marry again, for the Mi'kmaq could see no reason why two people should be unhappy. Usually a Mi'kmaq had only one wife, but because of the great need for children that the life of the nation should go on, and for other reasons, a good hunter sometimes had as many wives as he could provide for. The first wife to bear a son was the mistress of the wigwam.

Sickness and Death

Sickness, recorded Lescarbot and others, was rare among the Mi'kmaq, but when they were sick they had remedies, which with the sweat bath, they had found helpful, and when these failed they sent for the medicineman. He made invocations to his spirit, blew upon the part injured, licked the body, made incisions and sucked the blood and applied slices of a beaver's kidney. When he had done all that he could he was given a present of venison or skins and went his way. If the patient could not live the Indians laid him on a bed of spruce boughs, and when he had drawn his last breath they covered his body with soft skins or with a robe of beaver, and with cords of leather or of bark they bound his legs flexed against his breast, his chin touching his knees. As his friends and relatives prepared his body for burial, others beat upon the bark of his wigwam, crying, *"oui, oui, oui,"* to make his soul come forth, and young men went near and far to tell of his death and to bid all who knew him to the burial. His body bound in skins was carried on a bier of bark to a common burial ground and was placed in a round hole, four or five feet deep, lined with twigs of fir and cedar and with gifts of bows and arrows, and snowshoes, quivers, and beads, and clothing, that the spirits of these things might go with him into the land of souls and be of service to him there. The chief and the old men formed a circle around the grave and the burial was made in silence except for the weeping and wailing of the women. The grave was filled with earth and covered with logs, and the Indians turned away at the chief's command to partake of the feast for the dead, to hear the funeral oration, and to take part in the songs and the dances, all of which were to celebrate the joy of the departed in meeting with his friends in the Land of Souls. During the time of mourning the Indians smeared their faces black and cut the ends of their hair and let it fall loose and unadorned. When a death occurred in the winter or when the Indians were far from their burial ground, the body, wrapped in birch bark painted black and red, was placed in the branches of a tree or on a high scaffold and later was interred and the grave marked with a symbol of the deceased: bows, arrows, a shield for a man; spoons, beads, ornaments for a woman.

Religion

The Mi'kmaq wove their religion around the world they lived in, around the mysterious forces they felt stirring within themselves, shaping their lives and directing their destinies. The Sun they believed was their creator. They called him Niscaminou – the Very Great. To him they gave their homage, devotion, and adoration, and because the sun governed all of nature, and ordered the world in which they lived, they bore with patience and great fortitude the adversities that came upon them, famine, sickness, the hardships of war, and the labour of fruitless hunting, believing these were the Sun's will. At sunset and at sunrise they turned their faces to the sun and cried, *"Ho, ho, ho,"* bowed low, gestured with their arms lifted above their heads, and asked the sun to give them the things they needed and desired: good hunting, protection for their families, power over their enemies, many offspring, and a long life. When famine came and there was great suffering the medicineman put on his sacred robe and, turning to the east, said, "Our Sun, give us something to eat." The Mi'kmaq prayed also to the moon, who, they believed, with the sun, had made them spring out of the earth. They asked her to protect them from the malignant night air, and to guide them in the hunt, and on nocturnal journeys, and to give to their women strength to bear many children and the ability to nourish them.

The meaning of life and of death was pondered by the old Mi'kmaq. They believed the body was animated and made whole by vital life, *memajoookun.* At death *memajoookun* left the body and became a soul, a spirit, a black shadow-image of the body it had animated. For a time at least after death the spirit lingered near friends and relatives, and at their feasts the Mi'kmaq put aside a portion of food for the souls walking near their wigwams. In the spirit land the spirit was bad or good as it was when it had animated the body. The bad spirit leaped and danced with great violence, and had to eat the bark of rotten trees as long as Papkootparou, the keeper of the Land of Souls, commanded. The good spirits lived a gentle life far from the noise of the wicked. They ate what they pleased, and for their enjoyment they hunted the souls of moose and of beavers with the souls of the bows and arrows which their friends and relatives had been careful to place in their graves. The Land of Souls was in another land, where there was an abundance of everything and where no one had to work. Still another belief was, that when they died they went up to the stars and afterwards into green meadows full of flowers and rare fruit. The Milky Way to the Mi'kmaq was the Spirit's Road.

Manitoo or *mundoo* was the mysterious power that the Indians felt permeated nature. From some event, or for some unusual feature of the land, or for some other reason *manitoo* was believed to dwell in certain places and in certain things, and at those places and to those things the Mi'kmaq gave their homage that the spirit of *manitoo* might be favourably inclined toward them. *Manitoo* could span the chasm between this world and the Land of Souls and, through the medicineman, who with ceremonial ritual had put himself into the power of the *manitoo*, could make the dead appear to tell the Indians of distant events, to advise them as to what they should do, and to forewarn them of danger, and to inspire them to seek revenge for insults. An Indian's *teomul* or totem was his guardian spirit and resided in something which he possessed. His faith in the power of his totem and its ability to protect and assist him gave him courage to perform wonderful feats of strength and daring. Totems were usually an animal, a bird, or a flower, and there were clan and family totems as well as those for an individual. The symbols of their totems were worn about the neck, were painted on their canoes and on their wigwams, and were worked in beads or were painted on their clothes.

The Mi'kmaq had no knowledge of the causes of natural phenomena. He felt the seasons turn from warm to cold and warm again, he heard the crackle of thunder and knew the strength of the wind. He saw the moon wax and wane, the stars flow across the heavens, and sometimes he felt the earth tremble beneath him until he quivered with fear. For the rush of the wind, the rolling of the seasons, the trembling of the earth he knew no reason, and in his imagination he gave to these mysterious events anthropomorphic existence. He believed the changes of the seasons came with the turning of Coolpujot whose boneless body was rolled over with handspikes every spring and fall, to the east, to the west, his breathing bringing the warm soft days of summer, the bleak cold days of winter, depending upon the way he was turned. Thunder was the growling of Kaktoogwak; storms were brewed by the Storm-Maker, Tumilkoontaoo, a mighty bird whose wing strokes stirred the great wind, the rain and the snow into motion; and the land shook until the Indians trembled when Kuhkw moved beneath the earth. There were many more: Pine-Chopper who felled trees in the forest, Swift-Foot, and Wind-Blower, and the Megumoowesoo who was created from the sounds the Mi'kmaq heard in the forest that were beautiful and mysterious and terrifying because they could not understand why there should be ethereal whispers in a land of trees.

Glooscap

The greatest character in Mi'kmaq mythology was their culture hero Glooscap. He was the expression of all that they desired to be, as he was the embodiment of all their achievements. As with the culture heroes of other nations, the Mi'kmaq believed that Glooscap was created or had a miraculous birth and childhood; that he was invulnerable; that he did great deeds in their land, and that he taught them all that they knew: how to make bows and arrows, canoes, and wigwams; and that he showed them how to fish and how to hunt. Like all other culture heroes, the Mi'kmaq said that Glooscap did not die, but that he went away to return someday when the Mi'kmaq have great need of him.

The name Glooscap would seem to be from the Mi'kmaq words, *keloose,* good, and perhaps *nedap,* friend, comrade. This information came from an old Indian who lived in Barrington, Nova Scotia. He told me many tales about the old Indians and how they lived when he was a boy, but he never told me any legends. One day I asked him if he knew any stories about Glooscap. He was at once interested in the name but told me he knew no stories about him. A few days later I met him again and he asked me to repeat the name of the person I had asked him about. He listened closely. Then he said he thought I must have heard some stories about someone who was good to the Indians, a good friend, a priest perhaps, for the word *gloos* meant good. This was thrilling information. Since then I have asked many Indians about the word Glooscap. They do not think much about the origin of words, except perhaps in the meaning of their place names, but all have told me, "*Gloos* means good, and that's what he was, a good friend."

Meeting with the white man was not a happy experience for the Mi'kmaq. Their way of life was often miserable and was a long struggle with the forces of

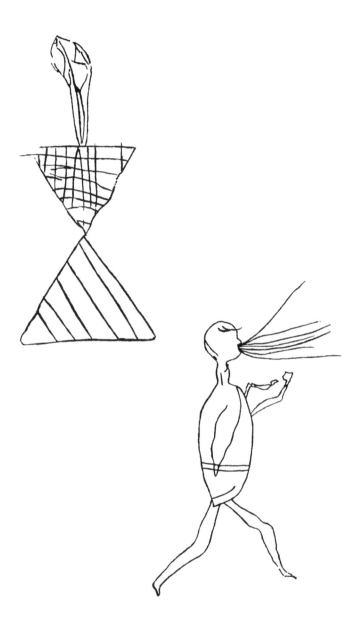

Thunderer and Windblower

nature — still it was their way and it was sweet to them. The land was theirs and had been theirs since the day they sprang from it, and when they saw it being stripped from them piece by piece they cried out, "Our Fathers lie buried here. Shall we say to the bones of our Fathers arise and go with us into a foreign land."

The Mi'kmaq strove long and fiercely for their land and for the way that was theirs, a struggle that was grossly unequal. Then, one by one, and in groups, the chiefs came to make peace with the white man that they might live untorn by warfare on the portions of land that were left to them. They came at first asking for great tracts of land, which they knew were large "but very moderate and very limited in view of the immensity of land they did possess." Then they came willing to live in peace on the land the white man offered, signing the treaties with the symbols of their totems, a bird, a fish, a flower, an animal, and accepting the white man's gifts of blankets and tobacco, powder and shot, golden belt and laced hat, agreeing, that, "the sun and the moon shall never see an end to our Friendship."

Many years have passed since the old Mi'kmaq signed their treaties with the white men who had taken their land. They have been hard years and lonely years with few of the white people remembering their plight. Today most of the Mi'kmaq live on reservations; a few live at the edges of towns or beside country roads near the woodlands their ancestors roamed. Their population, once shattered by the diseases of the white man, is slowly increasing until there are now several thousand living in the land that was once theirs. The men are excellent guides; many of the women good basket makers. Some have cleared land and do a little gardening; others work in the woods at lumber camps or work in the towns; a few have positions of responsibility in the world outside the reservations. Many of the young Mi'kmaq feel a growing need for training in occupations which require skill and specialized knowledge. As they acquire the proficiency they need in classes and in vocational schools and, as they turn to work away from the reservations, the old ways are being forgotten. But there are still many who speak Mi'kmaq, many who cherish the memory of the old days, and remember the old tales and traditions of their people.

TALES AND TRADITIONS OF THE MI'KMAQ

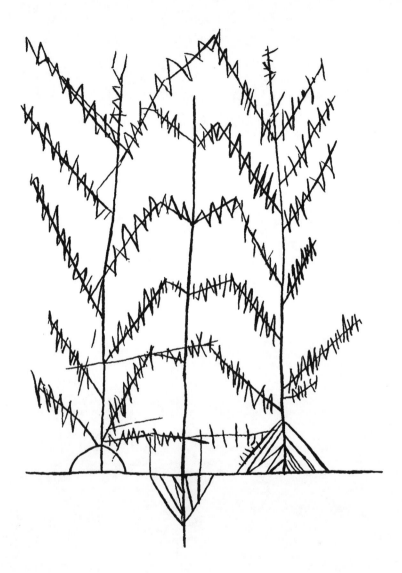

Three Trees

How Niscaminou Made the Mi'kmaq

Niscaminou, the Sun, the Very Great, made the sky and the stars, and flung the Great White Spirit Road like silver lace across the heavens. Sometime after he made the sky and the stars he made the earth, the tall trees and the flowers. He made the mountains to rise above the land and poured the sea into the hollow places. He made the rocks and the sandy shores. He made the rain and the fog; the snow and the dew, and the wind that moves over the earth. Then, after he had made the sky and the earth, the flowers and the tall trees, he made the Indians.

Reaching across the sky to the Moon following in his path as an Indian woman follows her Indian husband, he mingled his rays with her light and let their mingled beams sink into the earth; and out of the earth came men and women. They were red-brown like the red-brown earth; tall and strong; and were warm with the Sun's rays.

They were the first people on the earth and they were Mi'kmaq.

Niscaminou and the Squirrels of Blue Mountain

In the old days a great chief of the Mi'kmaq lived on Blue Mountain, near Kemptville on the Tusket River. When he was very old and had been a chief for many winters, Niscaminou came to his wigwam.

"Chief," said Niscaminou, "in this land of great chiefs I have found no one greater than you, nor have I found any Indians greater than your people. Because you are a great chief and because you have led your people with courage through good times and hard times I want to honour you. Whatever you wish that I will grant."

The old chief was pleased that the Great Creator wished to honour him and he sat in long silence and thought of the things he might ask of Niscaminou.

He thought of Earthquake who shook the land until a man could not stand, and he fell quivering into the broken earth. He would ask Niscaminou never to let Earthquake walk again in the land of the Mi'kmaq. But as long as he could remember Earthquake had not walked in their land, shaking the earth so hard a man could not stand. Earthquake was far away. He would not ask Niscaminou to keep him from their land forever.

He thought of the Great Thunderer and how his bright light sometimes killed a man. But in all his days he had never feared the Great Thunderer. He would not ask Niscaminou to keep Big Thunder always in his hills and away from the land of the Mi'kmaq.

He recalled the old tales of the mighty Culloo whose wings covered the earth in darkness, and the Indians crept into the caves and hid in the thick woods. But he had never seen the mighty Culloo, nor had he known anyone who had. Culloo was only in the old tales.

He remembered the winters when Ukwtakun, the hungry one stalked the bare land and there was nothing for the Indians to eat. But if a man ate the inner bark of trees and the lichens on the rocks he could live.

Then he remembered Death and that he was old. With a rush of joy he thought he would ask Niscaminou to let him live forever and ever. If he lived forever he would never lie on a scaffold of poles in the wind and the rain and the cold; he would never go into the earth. He would live with no thought of death; sleep and always wake. But when he looked up into the sky he knew he was not afraid for his spirit to go the way of the Great White Spirit Road.

It was then a squirrel came over the hills of Blue Mountain and the old chief scowled. (In the old days the squirrels were monstrous animals, stronger than the Indians who could not drive them from their wigwams when they came thieving in the villages; and nowhere in all the land of the Mi'kmaq were the squirrels a greater nuisance than in the hills of the Blue Mountain near the Tusket River). Now he knew what he would ask of the Great Creator.

"Niscaminou, make the squirrels so little they will never again be a pest to the Mi'kmaq." Niscaminou looked at the mighty squirrel; and he was a tiny animal, small like the squirrels are now on Blue Mountain and in all the land of the old Mi'kmaq.

Culloo

TALES OF THE STARS AND THE MOON

The Sisters Who Married Stars

In the old times there were two sisters who were known as the Weasels for their fair skin and because they were slender and graceful. One day their mother, who was a widow, sent them into the woods to look for *segubun,* the wild Indian potato. They roamed the woods all day until their baskets were full. When night came and they turned to go back to their wigwam they did not know which way to go. At last they lay down on a green bank of moss and, looking up into the sky, they wondered if far above them there were Indian people.

"The stars are like the eyes of warriors guarding the night," said the elder sister. "If the bright star in the west were an Indian warrior I would choose him for my husband." Then she added, "If that star is an Indian warrior I want to marry him."

"I," said the younger sister, "would choose the warrior of the little red star. If that star is an Indian I will marry him."

They fell asleep, and in the morning when the younger sister awoke and stretched out her feet a thin voice wheezed, "Careful there, you have upset my eye wash." She opened her eyes and there beside her was a wrinkled old man with sore red eyes. The little red star of the night had heard her choice and had come to be her husband.

When the elder sister awoke a husky voice called out, "Take care, you have upset my red ochre." The bright star of her choice sat beside her, and he was, as she had wished, an Indian warrior.

Near the sisters were two wigwams. They got up from the green bank of moss where they had slept and went into the wigwams as the wives of the stars. When their husbands left them to go hunting they were told to do as they chose, except that they were never to lift up a large stone that lay on the ground near the wigwams. The younger sister fumed and fussed about it.

"Why should I not touch it if I wish. It is only a stone." But the elder sister would not let her move it nor touch it. She pouted and complained about the stone and kicked it with her toes, and one day when she was alone she lifted it and peeped under. When she saw what was beneath the stone she shrieked in horror. Her sister ran to her, and when she knew what her sister had seen she pushed and pulled until they could see all that lay beneath the stone. They were in the sky and far below them was the earth. They wept and wept until their eyes were as sore and red as the eyes of the red star the younger sister had married.

When their husbands came from hunting the sisters tried to hide their grief; but their faces were marked with their tears and their husbands asked anxiously,

"What has happened to make you cry?"

"Nothing has happened," the sisters answered.

"But you are not happy," said the Stars. "Something has grieved you."

They looked at the stone and saw that it had been moved.

"Ah, you have looked beneath the stone and have seen the earth." The sisters wept bitterly.

"Don't cry," their husbands told them. "If you are lonely for the earth you may go back. Tonight sleep on the green bank of moss where you slept that night you chose us for your husbands, and in the morning you will be on the earth where we found you. But when you wake up in the morning do not open your eyes nor throw the blanket from your faces. Wait until you hear the Chickadee, and still wait until the Red Squirrel chirrs. Even then do not open your eyes until you hear the Chipmunk chatter."

The sisters slept on the green bank of moss and early in the morning they heard a Chickadee. The younger sister jumped up and would have tossed the blanket from her face if her sister had not made her wait to hear the Chipmunk chatter. The sunlight moved through the trees and made long shafts of light through the green woods. In the distance a Red Squirrel chirred. The younger sister could wait no longer. She sprang up to greet the earth; but the earth was not there. In her haste she had broken their flight and they were caught in the branches of a broad-limbed pine. She wailed bitterly,

"Why did I not wait until the Chipmunk chattered."

Her sister looked down the long bare trunk of the pine and told her hopefully, "Someone will help us down the tree trunk."

"Who will help us when we have nothing to give."

"We have ourselves," her sister told her. "Someone will want us to be his wives and keep his wigwam." They waited long and anxiously before Moose came thundering down the wood path. They called gaily to him, "Moose, help us down from this tree. If you will help us we will be your wives and care for your wigwam."

Moose looked at them with disdain.

"Why should I want you two Weasels for my wives."

When Bear came grumbling along the path the sisters called hopefully to him, "Bear, help us from this tree and we will be your wives. "

Bear looked up at the Weasels with disgust.

"I married in the early spring," he told them crossly, and ambled off through the trees.

The sisters were weary with waiting long before Marten came gliding through the shadows. They called anxiously to him, "Marten, help us down this tree. Help us and we will be your wives and care for your wigwam."

But Marten was not interested. He too had married in the spring. When the sisters saw Badger walking down the wood path they drew back into the branches of the pine and hid from his sight, for all their lives they had feared the wily Badger and his mean pranks. Still they were far from the earth and he might help them.

They called cautiously, "Badger, if you will help us down this tree we will care for your wigwam and be your wives."

Badger looked at them in scorn and walked away. Then he thought how he could amuse himself with the sisters, and he turned back, climbed the tree and helped the younger sister to the ground. When Badger came back the sisters knew he came to plague them, and the elder sister was determined that he should not tease her with his pranks. She took the long cord that she used to tie her hair, and bound it in knots about the branches of the pine. When Badger had helped her down the tree she cried innocently, "Oh, my hair string. I left it on the tree top. Get it for me Badger."

Badger climbed up the tree again while the sisters built a wigwam of boughs. They drew the sides neatly together, paved the floor with broken flints, and wove into the boughs a wasp's nest and a bundle of thorns. As they scurried about the elder sister called to Badger, "Don't break my hair string. Untie all the knots."

When Badger had the cord untied the elder sister whispered, "We will hide in the woods and when Badger goes into the wigwam we will call to him in the voices of the wasps and the thorns. We will be the pranksters, not Badger."

Badger slid down the long trunk of the pine and dashed into the wigwam and fell on the flints. He cried out and a sweet voice called, "Come here, Badger." He darted across the wigwam and was caught in the thorns. He shouted angrily and a soft voice whispered from the other side of the wigwam, "This way, Badger." He stumbled toward the voice and fell into the wasp's nest. In an ugly rage he dashed out of the wigwam. Never had anyone dared do to him what he did to others.

Far ahead of Badger, the sisters slid through the shadows until they came to a river where Crane stood to stretch his long neck as a bridge across the water. They rushed up to him.

"Crane," they panted, "help us across the river."

Crane lifted his long ugly neck and stared at them.

"Where is your fee?" he demanded crossly.

The sisters told him, 'We have nothing we can give you Crane, but we know you will help us for you are always so good and kind." "Indeed, indeed, good and kind," murmured the pleased Crane. "What beautiful feathers you have Crane! They are soft and smooth like thistle down. And your long legs! How beautiful and straight!" "Ah," breathed Crane, "my feathers smooth as thistle down. My legs straight and beautiful." Crane was an ugly old bird and the sisters chuckled to themselves as he preened his feathers and strutted along the river bank. They begged him patiently, "Stretch out your beautiful neck as a bridge Crane." "Indeed I will for two such beautiful girls," Crane told them, as he stepped down to the water's edge and stretched his long neck across the river. "But be careful of my beautiful feathers that you do not hurt them."

The sisters ran lightly across Crane's neck as Badger came panting out of the woods and demanded that Crane should help him over the river.

"Here old bird, help me across this river," he ordered.

Crane drew in his long neck and stared at Badger.

"Well, well, have you nothing to say about my beautiful feathers?" "Beautiful feathers!" exclaimed Badger. "You are the ugliest old bird on the river. There, help me across."

Crane pushed out his neck angrily.

"That I will indeed," he snapped. "But be careful of my feathers and walk gently."

Badger jumped on Crane's neck and ran with pounding steps until he came to the middle of the river. "Did you say be careful of your beautiful feathers?" he taunted with a kick that sent Crane's feathers flying. "There, that's for your fine feathers, old bird," he shouted gleefully. "And that's for you," snapped Crane with a sudden twist of his neck that sent Badger hurling through the air and into the river. Above the rumble of the water the sisters heard Badger shout,

Crane and Girl

"I want to go to Cajahligunuch," and they fled in a panic, for they knew they were evil words, dark with magic, and that wily Badger would live and would follow until he found them.

They ran on and on through the woods until they came to a river where they saw Loon and Scape-grace. They begged to go with them, and Loon and Scape-grace took them to the village of the Widgeon Indians, where they married two of the Widgeon chiefs. In their happiness they forgot the evil words that Badger had shouted. But they never forgot their home in the sky nor their Star Husbands.

Mooin and the Seven Hunters

Mooin, the Bear, the Mi'kmaq call the four stars of the Big Dipper, or the Great Bear, Ursa Major. The three stars of the handle of the dipper, or the tail of the Bear, they say are the first three of seven hunters who pursue the Bear across the northern sky during the warm summer months: Robin (because it is a reddish star), Chickadee (because it is small like a chickadee), and Moose Bird (Gray Jay). In the constellation Bootes are the four other hunters: Pigeon, Blue Jay (because it is a blue star), Owl (Koo-koo-gwesoo), and Saw-whet – the four that lose the chase as they drop from sight below the northern horizon in the late summer. Above the hunters is Mooin's den the group of stars of Corona Borealis. The tiny star beside Chickadee is his cooking pot which he carries along to cook the meat when Mooin is killed.

For generations on summer evenings the Mi'kmaq watched the four stars of the Bear fleeing across the northern horizon trailed by the seven stars, whom they called the seven hunters. In the cold moons of winter they saw the same four stars of the Bear lying high in the sky. Then, as the earth turned warm in the spring, they watched the four stars descend the steep slopes of the heavens and again flee across the northern sky. The tale of Mooin and the seven hunters is a very old myth of the Mi'kmaq and one which they told and still tell in the present tense because it is always happening.

In the spring Mooin in the sky awakes from her long winter sleep, leaves her den and comes down the steep hills to look for food. Chickadee sees her, but being little he cannot follow the trail alone and he calls for the other hunters. Together they start off with Chickadee and his cooking pot between Robin and Moose Bird. He is so little he might get lost in the great sky if Robin and Moose Bird were not there to look after him.

All summer Mooin runs across the northern sky and the hunters follow. But as autumn creeps into the summer nights the four hunters, Blue Jay, Saw-whet,

Stars

Owl, and Pigeon, far behind the others, grow weary, and one by one they lose the trail. First Owl, Koo-koo-gwesoo, and Saw-whet drop by the way. But you must not laugh when you hear that Saw-whet fails to share in the meat, and you must not mock his rasping cry, for if you do, wherever you are, he will come in the night with his flaming torch of bark and burn the clothes that cover you. Then, Blue Jay and Pigeon lose the way, and in the crisp nights of autumn only Moose Bird and Chickadee and Robin, the hunters that are always hunting, are on the trail. At last Mooin grows weary of the long chase and is overtaken by Robin.

Brought to bay, Mooin rears to defend herself; Robin pierces her with his arrow, and she falls dead upon her back. Hungry from the long chase, and always thin in the autumn, Robin is eager for Mooin's fat. He leaps on her bleeding body and is covered with blood. Flying to the nearest maple in sky-land he shakes off the blood – all except from his breast. "That," Chickadee tells him, "you will have as long as your name is Robin."

The blood that Robin shakes from his back spatters far and wide over the trees on the earth below. Thus, every year, comes the red on the leaves, reddest on the maples because the maple in the sky receives the most blood. The sky, as you know, is just the same as the earth, only up above and older.

After Robin kills Mooin, Chickadee arrives, and together they cut the meat and cook it in Chickadee's pot. As they begin to eat Moose Bird arrives. He had almost lost the trail, but when he found it again he did not hurry. He knew it would take some time for the others to cut the meat and cook it, and he did not mind missing the work. Indeed he was so well pleased with lagging behind and arriving just as the food was ready that he has ever since ceased to hunt and follows the hunters sharing with them the spoils of the hunt. "He-who-comes-in-at-the-last-moment," Mikchagogwech he is called.

Robin and Chickadee being generous share their meat with Moose Bird, and together Robin and Moose Bird dance around the pot as Chickadee stirs the meat. And so did the old Mi'kmaq in the old days when the Indians were brothers and shared their food.

All winter Mooin's skeleton lies on its back in the sky. But her life-spirit has entered another Mooin that lies on her back, invisible in the den, and sleeping the long sleep of winter. When spring touches the sky she will awake and come from her den, and will descend the steep slopes of the sky, and again will be chased by the hunters. In the chill days of autumn she will be slain, and will send her life-spirit into the body of a bear that lies invisible in the den. Thus life goes on from generation to generation. There is no end.

Moon Chief

Long ago, in the old times, there was an old man who could no longer go hunting. When he was young he was a great hunter and there was always food in his wigwam. Now that he was old and weary and could not hunt he and his wife were often hungry. One winter they had very little to eat; and at last, one cold night, there was nothing left, not even an old moccasin that they could chew. The old man knew that they could not live much longer. He said to his wife, "Look out the door and see if Moon Chief is out tonight."

The old woman crawled to the door and lifted the flap.

"Yes, Moon Chief is out," she told her husband.

The old man crept outside the wigwam and stood in the deep snow. He looked up at the moon.

"My friend, how are you tonight? We in our wigwam are not very well off. My wife and I have no food. In the old days you remember I was a good hunter. I killed the moose and the caribou and chased them through the deep snow. Now I am old and cannot hunt as I used to. Will you help me, Moon Chief? Send a moose here to my door,"

The old woman heard him talking. She called out to him, "What are you saying out there in the dark?" The old man told her, "I am asking Moon Chief to send a moose to our door." Early the next morning the old woman went to the door and looked out. Lying in a snow bank beside the wigwam was a big moose. She called out to the old man. "Wake up. Wake up. Moon Chief has sent us a moose."

The old man awoke, took his bow and arrows and killed the moose caught in the snow that lay against the wigwam. So it was in the old days if a man asked Moon Chief for the things he needed, believing that Moon Chief would give him what he asked for. To say, I will try Moon Chief, see if he won't send me a moose, will not do. Only if you feel you are bound to get what you ask for will Moon Chief send you whatever it is you need.

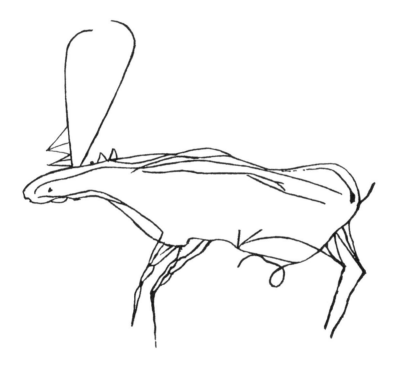

Moose

How the Loon Became a Sea Bird

A long time ago the loon was a land bird. He was a great nuisance to the Indians for he was always around, in and out of their wigwams, tumbling over their baskets, upsetting their firewood. The Indians shouted at him and threw things at him. Still he came poking around their wigwams, until one day he upset an old Indian's pot of beans.

The Indian grabbed him.

"Now I'm going to throw you in the fire, or I'm going to throw you in the water."

Loon squirmed and tugged to get away.

"Don't throw me in the water. Don't throw me in the water," he begged. "Throw me in the fire, but don't throw me in the water." "If that's what you don't want, that's what I'll do. I'll throw you in the water." The old Indian threw him in his canoe and paddled out into the deep water and tossed him over the canoe. Loon went off laughing, the wild laugh that he has laughed ever since at the Indians when he remembers the old Mi'kmaq who threw him in the water.

"Just what I wanted. Just what I wanted."

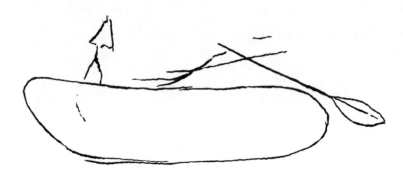

How the Bullfrog Got His Hunched Back

In a large Indian village lived Chief Bullfrog. He was a gruff and surly old chief and a wily magician. When he knew that Kitpooseagunow, the great magician of Partridge Island, and his brother were coming to his village, he stole all the water in the land, from the springs, the brooks, the ponds, from the rivers and lakes and stored it in buckets in his wigwam. The earth turned hard and dry; the leaves fell from the trees. When the Indians came grumbling to his wigwam he shouted angrily, "You ungrateful people. I take the water from the land to save you from the evil magician Kitpooseagunow and his brother and you complain. When they find the land a barren waste and no water they will turn back and you will be safe. But you shall have water. I have saved it for you. I will give you all you need."

The Indians fumed among themselves; but they were thirsty and they went humbly to Chief Bullfrog and he gave to each a small dipper of water.

Then came Kitpooseagunow and his brother. They saw the bare trees and the hard earth. They searched for water, and when they found none, they hurried on into the village and asked for some at the first wigwam.

The woman of the wigwam lifted her empty water pail and pointed across the village.

"Only in Big Chief Bullfrog's wigwam is there water," she told them. "Then," said Kitpooseagunow, "ask Big Chief Bullfrog for water." The woman sent her son across the village to Bullfrog's wigwam, and Bullfrog poured a little dirty water into his pail.

When Kitpooseagunow saw the dirty water he threw it on the ground.

"Go tell Chief Bullfrog I want clean water."

The boy went again to Bullfrog's wigwam and again his pail was filled with dirty water.

Kitpooseagunow was angry.

"Throw it away. It is not fit to drink."

But the boy's mother begged for the water.

"Let me save it for my son. There is no other water." Kitpooseagunow shouted angrily, "There is water. In old Chief Bullfrog's wigwam there is water fit to drink. Tell him I want water that is as fresh as morning dew."

Again the boy went across the village to Bullfrog's wigwam, and again his pail was filled with the dregs of dirt from the great bowls of water.

Old Bullfrog was gruff.

"Don't come again. I can't give you all the water in my wigwam." When Kitpooseagunow saw the dregs of muddy water he screamed like the north wind.

"I will get fresh water from old Bullfrog."

He strode across the village and into Bullfrog's wigwam. In a howling rage he grabbed old Bullfrog and bent him over his knee until his back cracked and was broken. He tossed him from the wigwam in a crumpled heap, and drove his spear into the great bowls of water hanging from the poles of the wigwam. In a torrent the water rushed out over the dry land into the stony rivers, and into the ponds and lakes, and again there was water in the land of the old Mi'kmaq.

Since that day, since Kitpooseagunow broke Chief Bullfrog's back, bullfrogs have borne a hunched back. The Indians remembering their old tales and how Chief Bullfrog stole the water from their land call a time of drought "a bullfrog moon."

Indian Corn and Tobacco

A very long time ago there was an Indian who lost his son. In his grief he knew he longed more for his boy than he longed to live. He decided, with others in the village where he lived, to go to the Land of the Dead and ask Papkootparout, the Keeper of Souls, for the soul of his son. They took their bows and arrows, their spears and clubs, and a bundle of long poles and started for the Land of Souls. They walked for days through an endless forest, and each night they pushed the ends of their poles into the earth for a wigwam and rested. At last, those who had survived the long way to the Land of Souls, saw the spirits of moose, and of beavers, and of dogs; and the spirits of canoes and of snowshoes which they knew were from their land of Gaspé, and from Miramichi and from Restigouche, and which were in the Land of Souls to serve the spirits of their fathers. They went on hopefully to find the soul of the boy they looked for, and came to the wigwam of a giant who shouted that he was Papkootparout, the Keeper of Souls, and no one could come into his land and live. Swinging his great stone club he lurched at the Indians. The boy's father ran to him.

"Stop! Papkootparout! Stop! Listen to me! These are my friends come with me to ask for the soul of my son. Listen Papkootparout! I had a son I loved more than I love life. When he was little I tucked my finger in his hand and he held it tight in his baby fist and I loved him then more than I loved anything in all the land. He toddled after his mother and cooed and laughed and there was nothing dearer than he was. He walked beside me in the hunt and lifted his first bow and arrow. Then, Papkootparout, the boy that I loved, died. He died, Papkootparout! My son died! I wept for him but the pain did not leave me; I grieved until I knew I must seek his soul in the land of the Dead. These my friends came with me, for they too loved my boy. Papkootparout, give me the soul of my son."

Papkootparout was touched with the man's grief for his boy and with the courage of the Indians to come into the Land of the Dead. He put aside his club, and promised to give the boy's soul to his father when he came into the land of Souls. "But it may be many moons," he told them, "before his soul reaches the land of the Dead. Let us roll dice while we wait."

The Indians staked their bows and arrows, their spears and clubs that they had brought from their land, and Papkootparout staked the seeds of corn and tobacco and fruit, the food of souls; and the game began. They tossed the little black and the white bone dice again and again; again and again; until at last the Indians were victors. Papkootparout gave them the seeds of corn and tobacco and told them to plant them in their land of Gaspé, and in the good earth of Miramichi and Restigouche.

The boy's soul now entered the wigwam, and the Indians heard the chanting of the spirits, rejoicing that a soul had come into the land of the Dead. They looked hard to see the boy, but there was nothing that they could see, not even the dark shadow that they knew was the soul after death. Papkootparout turned to the boy and commanded his soul to become the size of a nut which he took in his hands and wrapped in a bag and gave to the father.

"This is your boy's soul. Go at once to your land and immediately put it in your son's body and he will live again. You must guard the bag that no opening comes in it, for should your boy's soul escape he will be lost to you forever.

The man took the bag with his son's soul in it and tied it carefully to his girdle, and the Indians left the Land of the Dead and hurried to their land. They gave the seeds of corn and tobacco to the first Indians they met, who planted them in the land of Gaspé and in the soil of Restigouche and Miramichi; and the Indians had sweet corn to eat and tobacco for their pleasure.

But the father forgot the words of Papkootparout. When he heard the thud, thud of the dance of joy and thankfulness for their safe return, he gave the bag with his son's soul in it to an old woman to guard while he danced. It was a strange bag and the old woman was curious. She opened it and the boy's soul sprang from the bag and fled back to the Land of the Dead. When the father saw the empty bag he fell dead to the ground; and his soul followed his son's soul into the far Land of the Dead.

The Storm-Maker

Before the white men came to the shores of Mi'kmaq Land, an Indian family lived alone on a lonely bay. They depended on fishing for their livelihood, especially on the spearing of eels which they dried and used for soup during the hungry moons of winter. The eels and other fish were plentiful and were easy to take from the sea, until a storm swept over the ocean and lashed the sea madly. The gale lasted for days and days until there was nothing left to eat. At last the father told his two sons that they must go along the coast and look for fish that may have been washed ashore. One of his sons struggled out of the wigwam and forced his way over the rocks. It seemed as if the wind would flay the skin from his body, but he crouched low against the rocks and pushed on along the shore until he came to a long point of land that jutted far out into the sea. There he saw the cause of their trouble, for standing on a rock at the far end of the ledge was a mighty bird flapping his great wings, stirring the wind and the heavy sea. The Indian knew it was the great Storm-Maker, and that he must outwit him if they were to live. He clung close to the rocks and drew himself along the ledge. He shouted against the wind, "Grandfather you are cold."

"I am not," snapped the Storm-Maker, and flapped his wings even more fiercely. The Indian forced his way over the rocks a little nearer to the Storm-Maker.

"Grandfather," he shouted, "you are very cold."

"No," howled the Storm-Maker.

The Indian struggled a little closer to the end of the ledge. "Grandfather, you are cold and weary. Let me carry you to the shore. " The Storm-Maker stared at the Indian. "Come, Grandfather, get on my back." The Storm-Maker blinked hard. "Grandfather, let me carry you to the shore." The old Storm-Maker turned suddenly on the Indian. "Do that, my Grandson." The Indian folded the Storm-Maker's wings and gently lifted him to his back and carried him carefully along the ledge, feeling his way from rock to rock until he came to the last. He climbed it cautiously, then pretended to slip and let the Storm-Maker fall heavily on the rocks.

The Indian fell on his knees beside the old Storm-Maker. "Grandfather. Grandfather," he cried, "you are hurt."

He bent over the Storm-Maker and ran his fingers gently over his wings. "Grandfather, your wings are broken. If you will lie still I will bind them for you." The Storm-Maker lay very still, and the Indian bound his wings with long strips of soft leather. The great storm was over; the wind was as still as the old Storm-Maker. The Indians went far out to sea to fish and to spear the eels that they could now see clearly through the still water. All summer the Storm-Maker lay with his wings bound. The sea was calm and the wind still; the Indians fished and there was plenty to eat in their wigwams. But after a time a dirty scum spread over the still sea, and the Indians were as hard-pressed as when the wind blew, for now they could not spear for eels because they could not see through the scum, and the smell of the dead water drove them from the shore.

The young Indian went to the old Storm-Maker.

"Grandfather, your wings have long been healed," he told him, "but I have not unbound them for fear you would brew a storm so great we would all die. If you will promise never again to brew a mighty storm, but only blow a little breeze, I will unbind your wings."

The Storm-Maker promised never again to blow a mighty storm, and the young Indian unbound his wings. The Old Storm-Maker stretched his weary old body and flapped his wings gently; the scum broke in long ripples and washed away over the sea. The Indians went fishing and speared the eels in the clear water along the shores, and again there was food in their wigwams.

The old Storm-Maker has remembered his promise to the young Indian, and has never again brewed a mighty storm, nor has he lifted the sea into mountains. Sometimes he has forgotten and has flapped his wings too hard, but never has he made a storm like the wind storms of the old days.

TALES OF THE LITTLE PEOPLE AND OTHER STORIES

The Little People

In a valley of the Musquodoboit lived the Little People. A man who knew where they lived thought he would tease them. He pulled off his coat and shouted to them to come and fight with him if they dared. No one appeared and he sat down to wait. It was hot and dry and after a time he fell asleep. Hours later when he awoke he found himself bound hand and foot. He could not see the cords that bound him, but he could neither move nor free himself.

He called out, "Ho, there. Who tied me?"

A voice from the cliffs called back, "Neen. It was I."

The man shouted, "Ho! It was you!"

The voice on the cliff answered, "Neen. It was I."

"Then untie me," shouted the man, "and I will never tease you again."

The man lay very still. Soon he felt hands touching his hands and feet. He sat up and the cords were gone. He got up from the ground and walked off down the valley of the Musquodoboit. He would tell the Indians to leave the Little People alone.

And so they did, until, one day many years later, three Indians, who were hunting in the place where the man had insulted the Little People, decided to call to them.

They shouted, "Ho! Come to your prayers."

Down from the cliffs came a silvery voice, "Ho! Come to your prayers. "

The men called back, "Ho! Come and get your dinner."

The voice answered, "Ho! Come and get your dinner."

The men laughed and went down the valley of the Musquodoboit. And the Little People laughed.

The Three Brothers and the Little People

In a lonely wigwam in the woods lived three brothers. They were unmarried and one brother cared for the wigwam when the other two hunted.

One day a little man came to their door who was no larger than a child. He was cold and hungry and begged to sit by the fire.

The brother who was in the wigwam that day made a place by the fire, and the little man sat down and warmed himself and asked for food. The brother gave him a small portion and he ate it hungrily and asked for more. Again the brother filled his dish and he ate as greedily as before and asked for more.

There was little food in the wigwam and when the little man pleaded for more and more the brother told him, "No, I cannot give you more. There is only enough left for my brothers."

But the little man cried so pitifully that the brother gave him food until there was nothing left. When it was gone the little man disappeared, and the brother was left with the empty kettle. When the brothers came home they were angry. "You should have known he was one of the Little People," they yelled at the brother. "If he had come when we were here there would be food." The next day one of the other brothers cared for the wigwam. Near the end of the day the same little man came to the door and begged for food and to sit by the fire. He begged pitifully and the brother let him come into the wigwam and gave him a small portion of food.

"He shall not have all from me," he thought, "only this very small portion." The little man ate hungrily, and as before, begged for more and more, until the kettle was empty. Then he was gone and the brother was alone. "He shall not fool me," the eldest brother shouted angrily when he saw the empty kettle. "Tomorrow I stay in the wigwam."

When the little man came the eldest brother stood in the doorway. "There is no food for you today," he told him.

"There is food," said the little man.

"There is no food for you," said the brother.

The little man was angry. He pushed the brother aside and strode boldly into the wigwam.

"Give me food," he begged pitifully.

But the eldest brother would not listen. He seized him roughly to push him from the wigwam; but the little man was strong and he could not throw him. They wrestled and the brother was glad when he ran from him. He threw his spear at him.

"Do not come again evil one," he shouted, as he watched the little man with the spear thrust through him go up into the hills. He told his brothers, "We will not see the little man again. I threw my spear through him." But the little man came again and begged the brother to draw the spear from him.

"That I will never do," the brother told him.

"Draw your spear from me," pleaded the little man, "and I will take you to a place where you and your brothers may find wives to care for your wigwam." The eldest brother did not like the work of the wigwam. When he was promised a wife he drew the spear from the little man, and he led the three brothers up the cliffs into the deep caves where they saw many tiny women sitting in a circle, and above them a circle of tiny men.

"Here are wives for you," said the little man proudly.

The three brothers stood before the tiny women.

"Can you care for a wigwam?" asked the eldest brother.

The little woman of his choice chanted in the voice of the Little People, "I can care for a wigwam." "Do you know the roots of the forest that are good to eat?" asked the youngest brother of the woman he had chosen for his wife.

"I know the roots of the forest that are good to eat," she answered.

The other brother asked the tiny woman of his choice, "Can you make a good strong coat of moose skin?" "I can make a good strong coat of moose skin," the tiny woman told him. When the little women had answered, the brothers took them for their wives, and they and their wives left the caves of the Little People and went down the valley to the brothers' wigwam. But the wives were not faithful. When the brothers left them alone in the wigwam they were away, and when the brothers called to them, they taunted them from the cliffs with the words the brothers called to them.

RED EARTH

The Indian Who Became a Megumoowesoo

Far away in the deep woods lived the Megumoowesoos. They were strange, lonely Indians who played sweet music on the *peepoogwen,* and wore a single red feather in their hair. Sometimes when the Indians were in the deep woods they heard their strange, sweet music, and hurried away, for to listen to the haunting music of the Megumoowesoos was to be enticed into their wigwams and transformed into a Megumoowesoo. The Megumoowesoos could do much that the Indians could not—still, they did not like to be different from their neighbours, nor did they want to live alone in the forest far from the Indian villages.

But there was one Indian who was not like his neighbours. He listened to a Megumoowesoo.

In the old days, before he listened to a Megumoowesoo, he lived in a large Indian village with his grandmother in a miserable old wigwam. His grandmother grieved because their wigwam was old and miserable and her grandson lazy and deformed. But the young man did not care about their miserable wigwam or that he was lazy because he hated his ugly, twisted body, and because, when he did work, he thought of other things, – of the sound of the night wind stealing through the trees, and the look of icicles like pale amethysts in the moonlight.

One day when he was hunting with the other men he lagged behind, and when night came he could not find his way back to the village. He roamed for days until he fell exhausted. It was then a stranger found him and took him to his wigwam. In the night they sat about their campfire, and the stranger played on a *peepoogwen.* The Indian listened and was strangely moved by the sweet sounds that came from the *peepoogwen.* The stranger watched him as he played; the sounds grew dark and foreboding and the Indian trembled; and again the sounds were like the sweet murmur of the night wind. When the stranger took the *peepoogwen* from his lips the Indian knew him for a Megumoowesoo and he cried out, "Let me live with you forever."

The Megumoowesoo did not answer, but put away his *peepoogwen,* and they slept beside their fire. When morning came the Megumoowesoo tied up a great bundle of furs and food and told the Indian to take it to the village where he had lived. But the Indian could not lift it from the ground. The Megumoowesoo with a laugh that shook the tree tops lightly tossed the bundle to his own shoulders and guided the Indian to the edge of the village.

"Let this be our meeting place if you have need of me," the Megumoowesoo told the Indian as he turned back into the woods.

The Indian walked into the village and was amazed that he had been gone a year. The Indians crowded around him and demanded to know where he had been. He did not like to tell them of the Megumoowesoo, and that he had lived in the wigwam of one, and so he answered boastfully.

"For many moons I have been hunting in the woods, I have killed moose and muskrats and fat beavers, and have dug the roots of *segubuns*. Go get my bundle where I left it at the edge of the woods." When the Indians found his pack there was not one among them who could lift it from the ground. They broke it open and carried it in portions to old Grandmother's wigwam. She was elated. She sat in the wigwam door where all could see her and pursed her thin old lips.

"My grandson is a mighty hunter. We lack nothing in our wigwam." Now that there was plenty in the wigwam and, a grandeur such as they had never known before, the young man forgot his ugly, twisted body and that he was a lazy hunter. He thought of a wife and said to his old grandmother.

"Come, now, Grandmother, make an evening visit."

Old grandmother chuckled, "Where shall I make an evening visit, Grandson ?"

"At the chief's wigwam," answered her grandson.

Old Grandmother made her way across the village to the chief's wigwam. "Chief," said old Grandmother, "my grandson and I are weary of living alone as we do, and I am growing old and feeble and can no longer care for our wigwam." The chief scowled at old Grandmother.

"Your grandson is lazy. When all is gone in your wigwam you will be as poor and as hungry as before." Old Grandmother trudged wearily home. But her grandson was unconcerned with the chief's answer. "Never mind, Grandmother. Some night old chief will make us an evening visit." Not long after this he left his grandmother's wigwam and went in search of the Megumoowesoo who was waiting as he had promised at the edge of the village. They walked into the deep woods to the wigwam of the Megumoowesoo, and again the Megumoowesoo played the *peepoogwen* and, as before, the Indian was enchanted. The Megumoosesoo watched him as he played, and he saw that the Indian yearned for sweet music.

He drew the *peepoogwen* from his lips.

"Do you, too, play sweet music on the *peepoogwen?*"

When the Indian told him he could not play, the Megumoowesoo passed the flute to him; and when he lifted it to his lips and placed his fingers over the stops he too could play the *peepoogwen*. As he played he forgot that he was ugly and scorned by the Indians, for all that he longed for came in sweet spirals of sound from the *peepoogwen*.

He remained two nights with the Megumoowesoo and then was told to go back to his wigwam. Again the Megumoowesoo tied up a great bundle of furs and food. But now the Indian could carry the great bundle on his own shoulders, for he was no longer an ordinary Indian, but a Megumoowesoo.

When he entered the village the Indians paused in their work to look at him, for no one had seen such a huge bundle since the lazy young man of their village had returned from his year in the woods. But no one knew him, and he went on to his grandmother's wigwam.

Old Grandmother was as brown and withered as an old leaf. When he entered she searched his face eagerly with her old eyes, and shook her head sadly.

"You are not my grandson gone so many moons hunting in the woods. "

The young man shouted for joy, for now he knew he was changed.

"It is I, Grandmother, no longer a lazy, ugly man, but a Megumoowesoo."
Old Grandmother cackled. In all the village there was not a grandmother with a grandson like hers, and it did not take her long to tell her neighbours of the wonderful thing that had happened to her grandson. Young and old flocked to the wigwam and stood in amazement about the handsome young man who had been ugly and twisted.

When evening came he played on the *peepoogwen,* and the Indians were entranced with his music. They marvelled that such sweet sounds could be drawn from an alder, for the flute was cut from the stem of an alder not quite as long as the Indian's arm, and from the six holes drilled into the wood came the sweet sounds that held them speechless. The young women of the village, dressed in their finest robes, now came to see old Grandmother whom they had never noticed when she was lonely and her grandson ugly and poor. But the young man turned away from their bold glances, and they were left alone with old Grandmother. Soon the chief came to make an evening visit. But his offer was turned aside with a shrug, and he had to return alone to his angry daughters.

Not long after the chief's visit the young man said to old Grandmother, "Come, now, Grandmother, make an evening visit."

Old Grandmother chuckled with delight.

"Where, Grandson, shall I make an evening visit?"

"At the far end of the village there is a poor wigwam where two girls live alone. Make your visit there." Old Grandmother tottered across the village and made her errand known to the two girls. To one she said, "Come, live in our wigwam." The girl asked humbly, "Is it your wish, too, that I come to your wigwam."

Old Grandmother was pleased.

"It is my wish that you come for my old hands are tired."

When the girls of the village heard of old Grandmother's visit they were angry. They would have been mean to the young girl if they could have found her. But she was no longer in the village, for the young man had taken her, and her sister, and his old grandmother far away into the deep woods where the Megumoowesoos live. Sometimes, deep in the forest, the Indians heard his strange, sweet, haunting music. But they never saw him again.

The Invisible Hunter

On the shores of a lake, near an Indian village, lived an Invisible Hunter. The Indians told many strange tales about him, about his prowess as a hunter and how he looked, but as no one ever saw him, no one could prove his tale. Many went to his wigwam and sat by his fire, and ate the food his sister gave them. They saw his moccasins when he drew them from his feet, and his coat when he hung it on a peg in the wigwam; but they never saw him. So many girls begged for a glimpse of him, that he at last said he would marry the first one who could see him.

All the girls in the village flocked to his wigwam to try their luck. They were greeted kindly by his sister and invited to sit by the fire. In the evening she asked them to walk with her along the shores of the lake and, as they walked, she asked, "Do you see my brother on the farther shore?"

Some said that they did; others answered truthfully.

Those who said they could see him, she asked, "Of what is my brother's shoulder strap made?" Some answered, "It is made from the skin of a young moose." Others said, "It is a withe of the willow." Or, "It is a skin of beaver covered with shining wampum." As they answered, she invited them back to the wigwam. When her brother entered the girls saw his moccasins when he dropped them on the floor of the wigwam; but they never saw him. In the far end of the village lived three sisters who had the care of their father's wigwam. The two elder sisters were rough with the youngest, especially the eldest, who made her do all the heavy work and often beat her and pushed her into the fire. When they heard that the Invisible Hunter would marry the first girl who could see him, the two elder sisters hurried across the village to his wigwam. In the evening they walked along the shore of the lake, and the sister of the Invisible Hunter asked them, "Do you see my brother?"

The elder sister answered, "I can see him on the farther shore like a dark shadow among the trees."

The other sister said, "There are only trees on the farther shore."

The sister of the Invisible Hunter turned to the elder sister and asked, "Of what is my brother's shoulder strap made?"

Girl in Birch Bark Dress wearing Leggings

She answered lightly with a toss of her head.

"It is a strap of rawhide."

"Come then," said the sister of the Invisible Hunter, "let us hurry to the wigwam and cook food for my brother." They hurried to the wigwam, and when the Invisible Hunter entered the sisters saw his moccasins and his hunting pack when he dropped them to the floor; but they could not see him.

The sisters went home pouting and were cross because they could not see the Invisible Hunter. When the younger sister asked for some of the shells their father had brought them to make wampum, the eldest sister slapped her and pushed her into the fire and shouted at her,

"Why should anyone as ugly and as covered with scars and sores as you are want wampum."

But the younger sister gave her a few shells and she made them into wampum and sewed them on an old pair of her father's moccasins. Then she went into the woods and gathered pieces of birch bark and made a dress, and with a charred stick she decorated it with the ancient symbols of her people. She made a cap and leggings, and dressed in these and her father's moccasins and her dress of bark, she walked across the village to the wigwam of the Invisible Hunter. The Indians laughed and jeered, "Look at Scars and Sores going to the wigwam of the Invisible Hunter." But the sister of the Invisible Hunter greeted her kindly and invited her into the wigwam. In the evening she walked with her along the shores of the lake, and asked her as she had asked all the girls,

"Do you see my brother?"

The girl answered, "Yes, I see your brother."

The sister asked again as she had asked all the others, "What is his shoulder strap made of?"

The girl answered, "His shoulder strap is a rainbow."

The sister of the Invisible Hunter laughed and drew her back to the wigwam. She dressed her in soft skins, rubbed her scars with an oil that left her skin without blemish, and combed her stringy hair until it shone and was long and straight and black.

"Go, now, sit on my brother's side of the wigwam, nearest the door where the wife of the wigwam sits." She who had been ugly and covered with scars sat in the place of the wife of the wigwam; and when the Invisible Hunter came, he sat beside her and made her his bride.

How Summer Was Brought Back to the Land of the Mi'kmaq

Long ago, in the old land of the Mi'kmaq, there was a village of twenty wigwams. High in the hills above the village lived the bears and the *gugwesk,* strange, tall people, covered with fur and with long hair hanging down to their knees. The people of the village worked hard; the men hunted for moose and for beavers and for all the other animals; the women cared for the wigwams and made baskets and moccasins and pretty cradleboards for their babies.

In one of the wigwams lived a father and mother with their five children, a girl, three big boys, and a little boy. After a time the father and the mother died. Their bodies were smoked, an old custom of the Mi'kmaq, and then were wrapped in birch bark. The little boy asked his sister, "Where is our father? Where is our mother?" His sister told him, "Our father and our mother have died. We will never see them again." The little boy cried bitterly. He cried and cried for two long days until the sister told her big brothers to go up in the hills and ask one of the lady bears to come down to stop their little brother from crying. One of the brothers went up the hill and found a lady bear. He told her, "Our baby brother is crying for our father and mother. Come help our sister to quiet him."

Lady bear left her two baby bears in their camp and went down the hill with the brother. She picked up the little boy in her arms and cuddled him and sang,

> "Ba – ba – bo,
> Ba – ba – bo."

She rocked him gently, crooning,

> "Ba – ba – bo,
> Ba – ba – bo."

The little boy stopped crying and fell asleep. But in the morning when he woke up he started to cry again. Lady bear told his brothers to make him a little bow and arrow to play with. Still the little boy cried. It was winter time and cold and the little boy shivered as he cried. At last the lady bear asked him what he would like to have to make him stop his crying. The little boy told her, "If you could make it summer again and warm like it was I would not cry."

Lady bear told his three brothers, Blue Jay, Loon, and Otter, "It is summer your little brother wants – the little birds and the flowers and the warm days. Take these big bags of hide and go west until you find warm weather. When you find it ask Sky to give you the hot air to bring back with you."

The three brothers started off towards the west. After a time they got to a place where it was very hot. They opened their bags and held them up to the sky. "Sky," they called gently, "fill our bags with hot air that we may take it back to our land." They heard someone say, "There, close your bags quickly. Now go to my wigwam. Take a pair of birds of all kinds, take some plants, and go back to your land. When you get there open up your bags and all my nice hot air will be in your land. When the snow is gone let the little birds go. Wherever you are there will never be any snow. It will always be summer."

When the boys got home to their wigwam they opened the bags. The snow melted and the land turned warm with summer. They put out the summer birds: the robins, the swallows, and the little song sparrows, and all the other birds of the warm days, and they went off in the trees singing. The brothers planted a garden for the little boy, and when the pretty flowers began to bloom he laughed.

Lady bear laughed with the little boy.

"Now I can go home to my baby bears," she told the brothers and the little boy's sister. "Your brother will not cry now that summer is in the land."

TALES OF THE GREAT GLOOSCAP

How Niscaminou Made Glooscap

Long ago, on the great bold cliffs of Cape North, on the eastern side of the Cape, Niscaminou—the Very Great, made Glooscap of the good red earth of Cape Breton, and breathed on him until he lived. Then, when he had made him and he breathed, Niscaminou willed that Glooscap should wait on the lonely cliffs seventy times seven days until he came again.

"Until I come, wait on this mountain," Niscaminou told Glooscap; and Glooscap waited, lying on the cliffs as Niscaminou had made him, with his head toward the rising sun, his feet toward the setting sun; his arms flat on the earth and stretched toward the south and the north.

He waited through long dark nights when the lone gull cried; he waited through the long, brittle-dry days of summer, and in the snow of winter. The wind came and the rain; still he waited. The hills turned from palest blue to indigo and were black and bare before the snow covered them with white. Still Niscaminou did not come; and Glooscap waited. The land turned soft with spring; the sea birds laid their eggs. Still Glooscap waited. Then, at noonday, when the red cliffs were blue with harebells, Niscaminou came again to Cape North, and from the dew that clings to rocks he made an old woman to care for Glooscap's wigwam. "Noogumich, Grandmother," Glooscap called her.

Still Niscaminou willed that Glooscap should wait on the great bold bluff of Cape North until the noon of another day, when he came again to the mountain, and from the sea foam where it was white and thick at the foot of the cliffs, he made a little man to wait on Glooscap. Nataoa-nsem, my sister's son, Little Marten, Glooscap called him.

Still Niscaminou willed that Glooscap should wait on Cape North, and with the next noonday, when the sun was high in the sky, came the mother of the Mi'kmaq out of the great beautiful earth of Cape Breton.

When Niscaminou had made old Grandmother, and Nataoa-nsem, my sister's son, Little Marten, and the mother of the Mi'kmaq, Glooscap left Cape North and went over the mountains until he came to Fairy Holes on the lovely bay of St. Ann. There he pitched his wigwam and lived for many long winters.

Glooscap and his Twin Brother Malsum

The old Mi'kmaq who lived near the St. John River said that Glooscap was born as were the Indians, and that he had a twin brother Malsumsis, Wolf the Younger, or Malsum, the Wolf. In their traditions and in their old tales before Glooscap and Malsum were born, they talked together how they should come into the world. Glooscap chose to be born as the Indians; Malsum chose to burst through his mother's side. Glooscap was born; Malsum stirred and sprang through his mother's side and killed her.

When they were grown to young men and lived on the banks of the Kennebecasis, Malsum, one day, said to his brother, "You and I are not ordinary Indians. We cannot be killed with arrows and spears, but only by one thing that is secret to us alone. Tell me brother how you may be killed. "

Glooscap, remembering that Malsum had killed their mother, and that his spirit was evil, answered gravely, "Only can I be killed by a stroke from an owl's feather. And you brother, how may you be killed?"

Malsum told him, "Only by a blow from a fern root."

They hunted and fished and feasted together, and it seemed that Malsum had forgotten how his brother could be killed. Then, one day, he went into the woods and shot an owl, and with one of its feathers he crept up behind Glooscap as he slept and struck him a hard blow. Glooscap awoke and was angry with Malsum, and told him it was not an owl's feather, but only a pine root that could kill him.

Malsum sulked for days. Then he went hunting with Glooscap, and when they were in the deep woods he dug a pine root and struck him. Glooscap was stunned and lay on the ground as if he were dead. Then he sprang up, drove Malsum into the forest, and sat down by a brook and said to himself, "It is a good thing I did not tell him that only a flowering rush can kill me."

Hidden in the sedges, Beaver heard Glooscap whisper the secret of his life. Remembering how Glooscap did not like him to build great dams and hold the water over the land, he crept away into the forest, his black eyes shining, and told Malsum he knew the secret of his brother's life. Malsum promised to give him whatever he asked for if he would tell him the secret of Glooscap's life. Beaver pressed close to Malsum and whispered,

"Only a flowering rush can kill your brother."

Then he demanded in a loud voice, "Now I want the wings of a pigeon."

Malsum rolled with laughter.

"You with the wings of a pigeon! You flat-tail! You with a tail like a file!"

Beaver drew away angrily and slapped his big broad tail, and went to Glooscap and told him what he had done. Glooscap knew that now he must kill his evil brother, and he took a fern root and struck Malsum and killed him, and changed his body into the Shickshock Mountains that rise blue and cold in the land of Gaspé.

Glooscap and Mikchikch

When Pictou was a Mi'kmaq village of a hundred wigwams an Indian named Mikchikch lived there. He was ugly and old and dirty, and old and dirty was his wigwam. Sometimes one of the Indian women would look in at his door and she would tell the other women of Piktook, as the old Mi'kmaq called, their village at Pictou, "Old Mikchikch's coat is torn," or "Old Mikchikch's wigwam is dirtier than ever." But the women of Piktook had many things to do and they soon forgot Mikchikch, his torn coat and his dirty wigwam.

Then Glooscap came to Piktook and saw Mikchikch and his miserable wigwam. He called to him, "Ho! my uncle on my mother's side. "

Old Mikchikch was delighted that the great Glooscap remembered him as his mother's brother. He called out to Glooscap, "Come up to the highest seat in the wigwam my sister's son and sit in the place of honour."

Glooscap entered old Mikchikch's wigwam and sat in the place of honour and ate the food old Mikchikch gave him. When they had eaten he said to Mikchikch, "Come, my mother's brother, make an evening visit," which was an Indian way of saying, "Come, find yourself a wife. "

Mikchikch lifted his old face to Glooscap.

"Who would have me and who would live in this old wigwam?" Glooscap leaned over Mikchikch's miserable fire and looked into his old face. "Mikchikch, I will make you young again. I will make you a handsome young warrior."

"You will make me young again!"

"I will make you young again. You shall be a handsome young warrior. "

Glooscap took his coat and his leggings and his broad hunting belt, in which his magic was hidden, and put them on old Mikchikch; and old Mikchikch stood before him a handsome young Indian.

"Go," said Glooscap. "Go dance with the chief's daughter." Mikchikch stepped out of his wigwam and strode across the village.

He sat with the others in the chief's wigwam and tossed the white beans and the black beans, probed into a pile of ashes for a hidden ring, and threw the chief's bone dice with gusto. When the dancing began he boldly danced with the chief's daughter around and around the old woman who beat upon a piece of bark and grunted in an endless rhythm. On and on he danced until he remembered that he was still the old Mikchikch and clammy fingers of fear clutched him, He shouted in a frenzy, "It is enough," and fled across the village to his wigwam.

He told Glooscap, "I danced with the chief's daughter until I remembered that I am still old Mikchikch." "But you are not old Mikchikch," Glooscap told him. "You are the handsome young man I have made you. Go now and ask for the chief's daughter."

Old Mikchikch trembled.

"'The chief's daughter would not have me."

"You have not asked."

But Mikchikch was afraid.

"If I marry the chief's daughter, some day they will find me beneath the youth you have made me. Then they will kill me. I will stay here no longer. I will go from Piktook."

"Where will you go, Mikchikch?" asked Glooscap.

"I will go where they can never find me."

Glooscap pondered.

"You shall go, Mikchikch. But you shall not go as a man. You shall go as a turtle." Glooscap took his belt in which his magic was hidden, his leggings and coat from Mikchikch, and the old ugly Mikchikch stood before him. "Go now from Piktook," Glooscap commanded old Mitchikch. "But go as a turtle, not as a man. You may live on the land, but water will not drown you. Your way may be lonely, but no one can easily harm you. You feared youth; fear not to be a turtle."

Mikchikch as a turtle went out from his old wigwam, Mikchikch who had been a man and could have married the chief's daughter. He has roamed far from Piktook since the day Glooscap changed him to a turtle. Perhaps he has forgotten the old village and how he was a man in the old days. But the Mi'kmaq who remember the tales of their people have not forgotten.

The Call of the Loon

On the shores of a lonely lake in Newfoundland there lived, long ago, a number of Indians who were known as the Loons. They were, as any of the old Indians could have told you, at times Indians, at other times loons; at will they could be either loons or Indians. This they could do because their totem was the loon.

To find the Loons on the shores of their lonely lake Glooscap went far into the wilderness of Newfoundland. For long days and far into the night they talked together, the great Glooscap and the lonely Loons; and when Glooscap turned away to leave the shores of their lake, they pressed about him and begged to be his servants. Three times the chief of the Loons flew about the lake, dipping in his flight before Glooscap; three times he pleaded,

"Let us be your friends and your servants."

Glooscap listened to the chief of the Loons; then he stood tall and straight before him.

"Chief, I am your friend and the good friend of your people, and I want you and your people to be my friends. It is my will that you should be my huntsmen and messengers. I must go now to another land. If you need me, think of me, and call this cry that I shall teach you, and I will be with you."

Standing on the shores of their lake, Glooscap taught the Loons a wild, eerie cry, filled with the lonely spirit of the earth. When he left them, and they called in their desolate voice, they knew that he was with them.

The loons still call in the night and when the earth is still and dark before a storm. Their cry is lonely and filled with yearning. The white man says it is the lone loon crying in its loneliness to the spirit of a lost mate. But the old Indians knew that the loons were calling to Glooscap, and that Glooscap answered. If he still answers, they do not know.

Only the loons know.

The First Cedar Tree

Long ago there were no cedar trees in the land of the old Mi'kmaq. There were the pines and the hemlocks, the sweet-scented fir and the spruce. There were the oaks and the maples, the moosewood and the quivering aspen, and the white birch trees so lovely in the moonlight they made the Indians tremble. But there were no cedar trees.

How the cedar trees came to be along the river valleys and on the hills of the eastern woodlands is a tale of the old Mi'kmaq.

Sometime after Glooscap left the land of the Mi'kmaq seven Indian men went in search of him. They did not know the way to Glooscap's wigwam in the faraway place where he had gone, but they went toward the west until they came to a high mountain. They could not climb its steep sides, but Glooscap had told them that all who believed in him could find him, and at last one of the men found a way up the cliffs. When they reached the top they found the descent was even more difficult, for the heavy cliffs overhung the base of the mountain. But again one of the Indians found a way, and the others followed into a narrow path guarded by two serpents whose venomous tongues swept the passage in angry darts. The seven waited; the serpents flicked back their tongues into their gaping jaws; the seven dashed through the pass, and saw before them a wall like a heavy cloud that rose and fell, grinding to bits all caught beneath it. Again the seven waited; the cloud rose in a rumbling clatter; they darted beneath it and were in Glooscap's land. It was bright and lovely and was filled with sunshine as Glooscap had told them it would be. Before them stood three wigwams: Glooscap's, and Coolpujot's, the boneless one whose breathing brewed storms and the passing seasons, and Kuhkw's, rumbling Earthquake, who had left the land of the Mi'kmaq to be with Glooscap.

Glooscap was elated when he saw the seven Indians for he knew the way was long and dangerous, and that only those who believed in him could find a way over the mountain, through the narrow pass, and under the hanging cloud of mist. The seven sat with him and smoked his sweet-scented tobacco, and to each he offered to grant a wish. To one he gave a potent medicine; to another, skill in hunting; to others, charm and grace of manner. At last there was but one Indian left, and when he was alone with Glooscap he did not know how to ask for the thing he most desired.

Glooscap asked him, "What is your wish?"

The man said, "Of all the lands I have seen there is one lovelier than all others. It is there I would live forever."

Glooscap leaned forward and looked at the man.

"You say, a land lovelier than all others."

The man answered, "A land lovelier than all others."

Glooscap asked, "What is that land called that is lovelier than all others? "

The man said, "It is called Megumaagee – the land of the Mi'kmaq." "Ah, Megumaagee, Megumaagee," murmured Glooscap. "The good land of the Mi'kmaq, the true red men. It is indeed a land of beauty; a land to live in forever."

But Glooscap was puzzled how he could grant the man's wish until he thought of a way that he could be carried into the land of the Mi'kmaq. He called Earthquake, and at his command, he took the man and stood him before Glooscap. But he was no longer a man; he was a cedar tree.

All summer the wind came gently through the cedar, and its branches murmured in a green whisper. When fall came Glooscap took his stone handspikes and turned Coolpujot toward the west. The soft days of summer were gone; it was autumn and chilly. The wind came roughly through the cedar and broke its wide branches. In the dark days of November Coolpujot brewed a thunder storm that tore the cedar until its limbs were driven from its trunk, and its seeds were carried by the wind far into the land of the Mi'kmaq. Where the seeds fell grew cedar trees, red-barked like the red-skinned Mi'kmaq who wanted to live forever in the land that is lovelier than all others.

Glooscap's Footprints

Along the shores of Meteghan, above the Fundy tides, are the rocks where Glooscap and his dogs walked and left their footprints pressed in the stone. This was when Glooscap was old, for beside the rough print of his moccasins is the mark of his cane, – there, and there, and there. From his footprints in the hard stone the Indians know that Glooscap was a mighty Indian, even when he was old and weary and walked with a cane. The Mi'kmaq have no tales why the great Glooscap was in Meteghan and walked along the shores above the Fundy tides. Only do they know that he was there, and that he left his footprints in the stone.

The Bird Islands

In the old times when Glooscap lived at Fairy Holes on St. Ann's Bay there was an evil wizard who did not like him. He was jealous of Glooscap because the Indians marvelled at Glooscap's magic, and took no heed of his. When the Indians passed his door on their way to Glooscap's wigwam, he sat beside his miserable little fire and prodded it angrily and mumbled to himself, "Glooscap. The great Glooscap."

He plotted slyly to kill Glooscap; but there was no way he could touch him. He tried to outwit him with his magic; but Glooscap eluded him. At last, one day, when Glooscap was away from Fairy Holes, he stole two girls from their wigwam and drove them mercilessly over the shore to St. Ann's Bay. The girls stumbled and fell on the rocks and he struck them with his spear.

"Your great Glooscap," he snarled at them, "where is he? Why has he not come to save you as he has said he would?"

He prodded them with the sharp point of his spear.

"Why do you not answer? Where is your great Glooscap? Perhaps if I shout for him he will come."

"Glooscap," he shrieked, "Glooscap."

The hills rang with his shrill jeers.

"Glooscap. Glooscap. Where are you, Glooscap?"

He screamed at the girls.

"Your Glooscap is a liar. When you need him he does not come." Then he saw the great Glooscap striding down the St. Ann shores. In a frenzy he struck the girls and drove them over the rocks. Lying on the shore he saw Glooscap's great stone canoe. He pushed the girls into it and heaved it into the deep water.

"What will you do now, Glooscap?" he jeered. "How will you save these girls?"

He paddled leisurely along the shores hurling scorn at Glooscap. "Ah, the great Glooscap," he taunted, "the great Glooscap."

He turned to laugh at Glooscap helpless on the shore; but Glooscap was beside him. With an ugly snarl he lurched at him and struck him with his paddle. Glooscap pushed him aside, set the girls carefully ashore, and turned on him, lifted him high above the bay and dropped him into the sea. The water rose and fell against the land and rolled back into the sea, and Glooscap turned to his broken canoe, pulled its shattered gunwales apart and left is as two islands, the Bird Islands. The wind, the rain, and the sea have beat against the islands until there is nothing left of the old smooth contours of Glooscap's great stone canoe. The sea birds long ago found the islands and still lay their eggs on the bare rocks. All day their hoarse cries echo against the shores, as lonely and as desolate as the sea that rises and falls against the broken rocks of Glooscap's old stone canoe.

How Glooscap Left the Mi'kmaq

After the white man came to the land of the old Mi'kmaq and made it their land, Glooscap left for his faraway home in the west. Before he left the Mi'kmaq he made a feast for the animals on the shores of Minas. He told them of the land where he was going, and when they had feasted he stepped into his canoe and, singing as he went, he glided over the russet waters of Minas. The animals watched until he was gone and his voice had faded into the silence. They turned away from the shores and, as they turned away, they found they no longer spoke one language as they had when Glooscap was with them. They were afraid when they could not understand each other, and have never walked together again as in the old days of Glooscap. The Great Snowy Owl went far into the dark woods where he still grieves for Glooscap. *"Koo-koo-skoos! Koo-koo-skoos!* Oh, I am sorry! Oh, I am sorry!" he mourns over and over.

At Cape d'Or, where he spent his last winter with the Mi'kmaq, Glooscap called the Indians to his wigwam. He told them, as he had told the animals, of the land where he was going and that he must go because the white man had come to their land. They begged him to stay, for they could not believe that the strange white man would take all of their land. But he turned away, touched his wigwam changing it to stone, and took old grandmother in his arms and carried her over the land to the north where he put her down as a mountain telling her that when he reached his home in the west she would be there. Then he went to Spencer's Island where he ate his last meal in the old land of the Mi'kmaq, and where he left his cooking kettle overturned as a small, round island. The scraps from his kettle he scattered along the shore and changed them to rock; his two dogs, still sitting on their haunches, he turned to stone and left them to guard his old cooking kettle.

From Spencer's Island Glooscap stepped across the water to Blomidon, and standing on the great bold cliffs he chanted thrice, "Let the small fish look at me."

Again, "Let the small fish look at me."

And again, "Let the small fish look at me."

A small whale came into Minas Channel and close in under the cliffs of Blomidon.

"What is it, Grandson?" he called to Glooscap.

"Glooscap knelt on Blomidon and called down the red bluff, "Grandfather, you are too small to carry me to the far land where I go. I need a mighty whale to carry me into the waters of the far west."

The whale turned from Blomidon and Glooscap chanted again, "Let the small fish look at me."

"Let the small fish look at me."

And again, "Let the small fish look at me."

A great whale came into the Minas waters close in to Blomidon. "Little Grandson," he called to Glooscap, "what is your wish?" Glooscap shouted down the cliffs, "Grandfather, I want to go to a far country."

The old whale bellowed, "Then get on my back little Grandson." Glooscap went down the steep cliffs of Blomidon and climbed on the broad back of the whale. The whale turned and plunged in the red water of Minas and circled into the blue Fundy tide. He went on and on until he was weary and asked anxiously, "Is not the land as a bowstring, little Grandson?"

Glooscap answered, "No, Grandfather, the land is far away."

The old whale pushed on. Soon he asked again, "Is not the land as a bowstring, Grandson?"

"No, the land is far away, Grandfather."

"But there are pebbles and shells beneath us," worried the whale. The land

was near, but Glooscap wanted the whale to carry him close to the shore, and he told him carelessly, "It is only a reef, Grandfather."

The old whale dashed on and ran his head far up on the shore.

"My Grandson," he groaned, "you have killed me."

"Not at all, Grandfather," Glooscap assured him as he leaped ashore and gave the whale a mighty shove with his hunting bow. "There, Grandfather," Glooscap panted, "why could you not trust me?"

The old whale rolled in the water.

"Little Grandson," he called back to Glooscap, "have you not an old pipe to give me?" Glooscap took his pipe and filled it with red willow bark, lit it and put it in the old whale's mouth. The whale drew away from the shore, and Glooscap watched until he could see only the faint puffs of smoke rolling up against the blue sky. Then he turned and strode across the hills. When he reached his faraway home there were Grandmother and Little Marten waiting in his wigwam; and nearby were the wigwams of Earthquake, and Coolpujot, the boneless one, who had left the land of the Mi'kmaq to be with him. There they still live in Glooscap's land and brew the fine and the stormy weather and the passing seasons that sweep over the old land of the Mi'kmaq.

The years have been long since Glooscap left the Mi'kmaq. Some of the Indians have forgotten that he ever lived in their old land; some have never heard of him. But a few remember and are faithful in their thoughts to the great Glooscap.

Insignia of a Chief

TALES AND HISTORICAL TRADITIONS

The Great Chief Ulgimoo

In the very old days the Mohawks and the Mi'kmaq lived in peace with each other. But after a time they quarreled, and the son of a Mohawk chief killed the son of a Mi'kmaq chief. Then there was no peace in the old land of the Mi'kmaq, nor in the land of the Mohawks, for neither the Mohawks nor the Mi'kmaq wished to forget their grievances.

For years they fought, killing and burning and laying waste the villages and the lonely wigwams. It seemed as if there would never be any great men among either the Mohawks or the Mi'kmaq who could lead their people into peace, for it takes great men to make peace, and the Mohawks and the Mi'kmaq had only great warriors. But after a time there arose among the Mi'kmaq a warrior-chief, named Ulgimoo, who made an uneasy peace with the Mohawks when he drove them out of the land that is now Nova Scotia. First he drove them from the southern shores of the Bay of Fundy, where they had fled from their enemies, out across the rough Fundy waters to the shores of New Brunswick, and then on and on through the woodlands until they came to Montreal. Then he drove them from the shores of Minas Basin, and from the villages of Cobequid, and from Tatamagouche and Maccan, and from the bleak lands along the Northumberland shores, down into the marshlands of Cumberland, and along the Petitcodiac River to Salisbury. There he built a strong fortification and held back the Mohawks from passing along the tidal waters of the Petitcodiac into the southern lands of the Mi'kmaq.

Ulgimoo lived to be very old and his name became great. The Mi'kmaq told the tales of his valour around their campfires for generations. But even more than over the tales of his valour, the Mi'kmaq marvelled over Ulgimoo's death, for he died twice.

It was in the season of falling leaves, when Ulgimoo was one hundred and three years old, that he died first. When the leaves turned scarlet on the maples Ulgimoo told the Indians, "Soon, very soon, I shall die. But you are not to bury me in the dark earth. You are to build a high flake of maple poles, and leave me where the wind and the snow and the winter sunshine can fall around me."

The Indians could not believe that their great Ulgimoo was about to die.

"You cannot die Ulgimoo," they told him.

Ulgimoo held up his old brown hands with his pipe clutched in his fingers.

"I shall die with the falling of the last birch leaf," he told them.

When the Indians saw Ulgimoo's pipe grasped in his fingers they knew he would die, as he said, when the last birch leaf fell; for they thought that Ulgimoo knew the meaning of the strange symbols cut into the bowl of his pipe, and that the day of his death was carved in the symbols.

In the long brooding stillness of autumn the Indian women prepared their furs for winter use, and gathered the roots of *segubun,* the wild Indian potato, for the long cold moons when it is hard to get a living. Ulgimoo sat in the warm sunshine and watched the women at their work, and as they finished he prepared himself for death, and when the last leaf fell from the birches, he died. The Indians took his body and wrapped it in skins and a covering of bark, and put into his old hands his pipe filled with red willow bark and tobacco that Ulgimoo need not be in want of these in the spirit land. They placed his body, wrapped in the bark, on a high flake of maple poles; and in the lonely stillness of the woodlands they left him, and went up the long rivers into the deep forest where they pitched their wigwams for the moons of snow.

Ulgimoo was alone with the wind and the snow and the chill sunshine, and all winter he was motionless in the bark that covered him. But when the warm days of spring came Ulgimoo's spirit-life stirred his stiff old body and he lived again, and came down from the tall flake of maple poles and went into his wigwam to wait for his Indian friends.

When the Indians found the bark broken and Ulgimoo's body gone, they shouted angrily, "The Mohawks were here and have stolen Ulgimoo's body."

Ulgimoo came from his wigwam.

"The Mohawks were not here. I was dead, but I live, because my spirit-life lived."

The Mi'kmaq crowded around Ulgimoo, and they saw the gaping wound in his cheek where a hungry marten had feasted in the cold moon of snow, and they knew he had been dead. But they did not seek to know how Ulgimoo had come back to life, because they believed that Ulgimoo's power was in his pipe, as they believed it was his pipe that told him where the Mohawks lurked and the day when he would die.

The days grew warm in the forest and the Indians left the woodlands and went to the low Cumberland hills above the Tantramar marshes. Ulgimoo sat all day in the doorway of his wigwam and watched the blue shadows glide over the marshes and the Cumberland hills, and he knew a deep contentment. Now that he had known death the Mohawks were as naught, and the fears that held his neighbours he had forgotten. Now he knew that joy came from the earth, from slow moving shadows and the sweet scent of grass. He marvelled that he had lived one hundred and three years and had not known these things were sweet and were good in themselves.

When the Cumberland hills turned purple in the autumn sunshine, the Indians took their wigwams and went down to a place near Minudie. There Ulgimoo died.

Before he died he told the Mi'kmaq, "Tomorrow, at noon, I shall die. For a night you are to bury me in this red earth. Then you are to open my grave. The day will be clear and cloudless, and out of the clear sky will come a great clap of thunder. With that mighty clap my spirit-life will be restored to my body, and I shall come from my grave and will live with you forever and ever. I shall never know death."

The next day, as Ulgimoo had told them, he died when the sun cast no shadows. The Indians took his body to Amherst Point and laid it on the ground, and sat down around Ulgimoo to hear the old men of the Mi'kmaq speak.

"All our lives we have known Ulgimoo. He is the greatest of all great Mi'kmaq; the greatest who has ever lived. When we were young he drove the hated Mohawks out of our land; when he was old he told us where the Mohawks lurked when they came stealing back into this land that is ours. He has always told us where to find the ripest fruit, where to hunt and where to fish. Even this moon we have looked to Ulgimoo to tell us where to fish; where to find the ripest berries; and where to find the roaming moose. But Ulgimoo is dead. Let him be dead. Let him sleep in peace in the good red earth that gave him life. If Ulgimoo lived forever no great men would arise among us, for our young men would look to Ulgimoo and would not seek to know what Ulgimoo knows. Our tribe would perish if our young men did not seek to have wisdom of their own. Ulgimoo is dead. Let him be dead. Let us dig his grave deep."

The Indians grunted, "Let it be so."

When they had spoken they flexed Ulgimoo's knees beneath his chin, and wrapped his body in furs and bark and laid him in a round grave with his head toward the west, that he might forever face the rising sun, and covered his grave with a mound of stones. The dark night crept around them, and they were afraid because they had covered Ulgimoo's grave with stones.

All night they waited beside Ulgimoo's grave, and when the day came it was clear and cloudless as Ulgimoo had told them it would be. They waited. A great clap of thunder shook the earth and they trembled, for they knew that deep in the earth the great Ulgimoo lived again. But they did not lift the stones from his grave; and the thunder passed and fell on the distant Cumberland hills, and they turned from Ulgimoo's grave and left him alone in the red earth.

Wokun

In the old days of the Mi'kmaq the southwestern shores of Nova Scotia were called Kespoogwit, "land's end." Through the dark forest of old Kespoogwit, near its southern tip, flows a river which the Scotch settlers named the Clyde, which the old Mi'kmaq knew as Oonigunsuk, a "good portage," because it was a good waterway into the deep woodlands, to their winter camping grounds and to good hunting and fishing.

Into the waters of old Oonigunsuk runs a creek the white man calls Bloody Creek, but which the Mi'kmaq called Wokun for a knife lying on a rock beneath its brown waters which they could never reach, not even with the tips of their fingers. An old Mi'kmaq I knew saw it in his youth when he went logging for the English. He reached for it eagerly, but it lay just beyond his fingertips. He reached again and again, but his fingers could never touch it.

Then he knew it was the knife that had slipped from the hands of a dying Indian generations ago, and that it had lain on the rock for countless years before he saw it. He could see why even the fierce spring torrents could not wash it away, for it had become part of the rock; nothing could remove it. But why he could not reach the knife he could not understand. He tried again, but the water was deep, deep, deep. Yet he knew the water was *not* very deep. He leaned over the brown water and gazed in wonder at the sharp blade and remembered the story he had heard when he was a child and lived with his people on the shores of Lake Sebim.

They had told him, that, long ago, two Mi'kmaq men fought on the banks of the Wokun. They tore fiercely at each other with their knives, until one of them lost his footing and was driven into the creek. His bloody knife slipped from his hand and sank down through the water to a rock beyond his reach. He clawed and thrashed the water, but the knife lay just beyond his fingertips;

and he too sank down through the cold creek water and lay as still as the knife on the rocks beneath.

When his people came and found him lying in the creek they lifted his body from the water. But when they reached for his knife they could not touch it even with the tips of their fingers; and they went away in awe of that place and the mystery that held the knife beyond their reach.

Long years went by, and the Mi'kmaq named the creek Wokun for the mysterious knife which they could see but could never touch.

Magua of Refugee Cove

When the Mi'kmaq were masters of the land, Refugee Cove, on the shores of Cape Chignecto, was an Indian encampment where Magua and his wife lived in contentment until Magua saw a beautiful young Indian woman and loved her. He knew that a Mi'kmaq could not leave his wife unless she was willing to leave him and returned happily to her father's wigwam; but he longed for the other woman and was determined that he would live with her.

Together he and his sweetheart planned to cross the Bay of Fundy to the shores of the Annapolis Valley and to live there apart from the Indians. If he left his wife at Refugee Cove, Magua knew the Indians would discover he had deserted her before he could find a hidden valley where he and his sweetheart could live undisturbed. Pretending he wanted something from Isle Haute he took his wife with him to the island, and in the night, while she slept, he stole away, back to the shores of Cape Chignecto where his sweetheart waited for him in the black folds of darkness.

Feeling their way out into the Bay of Fundy they soon lost the bold cliffs of Chignecto; but as they passed Isle Haute the sea was bright with rising sunlight. From the shores of the island Magua's wife saw her husband and a strange woman with him. She climbed the steep cliffs and watched until they faded against the distant shore, her eyes blazing with anger.

Turning from the steep bluffs Magua's wife gathered the dry driftwood on the shores and heaped it high on the cliffs above. At nightfall she lit the great piles of wood and waited for the Indians of Refugee Cove to come in answer to her signal. At dawn she saw them moving stealthily over the water, their paddles lifted as they listened for strange voices. When they saw her and heard that Magua had deserted her they pushed off angrily from the island.

"We will find him if he has gone to the end of the seas," they assured her as they turned their canoes for the red Fundy shores. In the deep coves and inlets and along the high cliffs they looked for him; and at French Cross they found him with his sweetheart. Magua knew the hard code of the Mi'kmaq, but when they took him he went without protest to Refugee Cove.

The chief and his men sat in the moving light of their campfire. It had been many moons since a Mi'kmaq had deserted his wife for another woman, and it did not take them long to decide what they would do with Magua.

The old chief stood before his people.

"Magua knew that a Mi'kmaq may not leave his wife and live with another woman. He knew if his wife did not bear him children he could put her aside and marry someone else. And he knows that if a man and a woman are not happy together, and there are no children, they have only to tell their neighbours they no longer share the same wigwam to be free to marry someone else; and he knows that a good hunter may have more than one wife in his wigwam if he can provide for wives and many children. But a man may never desert his wife. If our men deserted their wives and children to tarry with other women we would perish from the land. Magua knew that among the Mi'kmaq desertion is death. Take him. Bind him and burn him in his canoe."

The Mi'kmaq grunted their approval and the young men took Magua and lashed him in his canoe, poured oil over his body, set fire to the canoe and pushed it off into the Fundy tides. Even Magua's wife in her anger shuddered as the flames leaped high above the sea; and his screams pierced her like a flight of arrows.

Memajoookun

Long ago, when the Mi'kmaq and the Mohawks were enemies, a Mohawk fell into the hands of the Mi'kmaq and was taken by a Mi'kmaq chief into his wigwam. The chief was good to his captive and made him one of his own family; but always he knew that his captive longed for his Mohawk people and for his land. At last he said to him:

"When you turn away from us and stare into the dark woodland are you thinking of your people and your land?"

The Mohawk's eyes burned with longing.

"To my land came the sweet days of spring; and I was not there. Summer covered our hills with berries; and I was here in this land. Now are the days when my people go up the rivers into the deep woods for the long moons of snow and ice. If I were in my land I would go up the long rivers into the deep woodlands that murmur and are still; whisper and are silent; as these woodlands murmur and are still but do not speak to me because I did not spring from this land."

The chief had a great love for the land that was his, and when he saw how his Mohawk captive longed for the land of the Mohawks, he told him.

"Tomorrow we will go far into the woods and peel bark for a canoe. We will build a strong canoe for it is a long way to your land." At daybreak the chief called. "Come, it is time to go. We have much to do."

The Mohawk went into the woods with his captor and all day he helped to peel bark from the white birch trees. He knew that this must be his last day, and that his captor had taken him into the deep woods to do what a chief of the Mi'kmaq must do to a Mohawk.

When night came his captor said, "We have some good bark but not enough. We will stay here tonight and get more tomorrow."

As they lay down to sleep the chief knew that his captor might kill him as he slept and he took his *memajoookun,* his soul, the bud of life, and hid it in the earth. Then he slept, knowing the Mohawk could not destroy him when he did not know the secret hiding place of his soul. But the Mohawk did not sleep, for deep in him he yearned to live. When his captor slept he killed him, tore his body into bits as was the custom of the Indians when they killed a hated foe; and in the darkness he vanished into the woods.

After a time the Mi'kmaq awoke from his sleep and found his body lying in pieces. He moved together as well as he could and his *memajoookun* entered his body and he lived again with vital, living life. He got up from the earth where he had slept and walked through the green woods rejoicing that there is no death if *memajoookun,* the soul, the very bud of life, lives.

MI'KMAQ INFORMANTS

Among the Mi'kmaq with whom I have talked I am particularly indebted to the late James Michael of Barrington, Nova Scotia, who was some seventy years of age when I talked to him thirty years ago in the 1930's. Although he spent many years of his life among white people he remembered and cherished his childhood with his parents when he lived in much the same way as the old Mi'kmaq of earlier years. Old Mali, who lived in Yarmouth County, Nova Scotia, at the time I met her in the 1950's, was a very wonderful old Indian. She had a fierce and loyal love for the old Mi'kmaq whom she remembered from the days of her childhood, for their way of life and for their way of thinking, above all for the Mi'kmaq language which she treasured and spoke dramatically. Julia Pictou and Abram Barlett, both of Yarmouth, Nova Scotia, know a good deal of the lore of the Mi'kmaq. From one I heard of Glooscap's footprints in the rocks at Meteghan; from the other the tale of the loon's wild laughter. To Neil Stephen of Barra Head, Cape Breton, and intelligent young Indian, I am indebted for information and for the Lord's Prayer in Mi'kmaq ideograms. To all my grateful thanks.

NOTES

The abbreviation *JAF* is for Journal of American Folklore. The motif numbers are those in Stith Thompson's *Motif Index of Folk Literature.*

CUSTOMS AND BELIEFS OF THE MI'KMAQ INDIANS

The information for this sketch on the customs and beliefs of the Mi'kmaq Indians is from the books listed in the bibliography, particularly from the writings of Lescarbot, Dièreville, Nicolas Denys, Father Chretien LeClercq, Father Maillard, and the Jesuit Fathers, and from conversation with a number of Mi'kmaq.

The Mi'kmaq were known by the early French settlers as the Souriquois, "the salt water men" according to Roth in *Acadia and the Acadians,* p. 27, to distinguish them from the Iroquois who inhabited the fresh water country. The name Mi'kmaq was first recorded in a memoir by de la Chesnaye in 1676. Professor Ganong in a footnote to the word *megamingo,* earth, as used by Marc Lescarbot remarked "that it is altogether probable that in this word lies the origin of the name Mi'kmaq." As suggested in this paper on the customs and beliefs of the Mi'kmaq it would seem that *megumaagee* the name used by the Mi'kmaq, or the *Megumawaach* as they called themselves, for their land, is from the words *megwaak,* "red" and *makumegek,* "on the earth"; or as Rand recorded "red on the earth" *megakumegek* "red ground", "red earth". The Mi'kmaq, then, must have thought of themselves as the red earth people or the people of the red earth. Others seeking a meaning for the word Mi'kmaq have suggested that it is from *nigumaach,* my brother, my friend, a word which was also used as a term of endearment by a husband for his wife. From this has come the interpretation of the word Mi'kmaq as meaning "allies". Marc Lescarbot referred to the word *nigamaach* when writing of the Indians of Florida whom he said had a word "which means

Brother, Friend, corresponding to Nigmach in the country where we dwelt." (vol. 3, p. 79). Still another explanation for the word Mi'kmaq suggested by Stansbury Hagar in "Micmac Magic and Medicine" (*JAF* 10:173) is that the word *megumawaach* is from *megumoowesoo,* the name of the Mi'kmaq's legendary master magicians, from whom the earliest Mi'kmaq wizards are said to have received their power, and from them the name was applied to the tribe.

According to one tradition of the Mi'kmaq their culture hero Glooscap, whom they share with the other Wabanaki tribes, was the youngest of seven sons of a *Megumoowesoo.* The Penobscot Indians call Glooscap, *Gluskabe,* a word which they say is derived from *gluski* "deceit, lie, nothing" with *abe* a stem denoting "person", and interpret it to mean 'deceiver, liar, or man from nothing', according to the different opinions of the informants. Dr. Frank Speck who obtained this meaning of the word *Gluskabe* commented (*JAF* 48:6) that the translation Deceiver or Trickster is not uncomplimentary as it refers to the ability to outwit one's enemies by strategy and cunning.

Tales and Traditions of the Mi'kmaq

TALES OF NISCAMINOU — THE VERY GREAT

How Niscaminou Made the Mi'kmaq.

These traditions of the old Mi'kmaq that the sun was the creator of the universe and that he made the Mi'kmaq spring up out of the earth are from statements recorded by Father Chrétien LeClercq in *New Relations of Gaspesia,* p. 143; from two Mi'kmaq prayers, one to the sun and one to the moon, recorded by Father Maillard: *An Account of the Customs and Manners of the Mickmakis and Maricheets Savage Nations, Now Dependent on the Government of Cape Breton,* pp. 22-25,47-48; and from Luther Roth: *Acadia and the Acadians,* p. 43. That the creator first made the heavens, then the earth, is from a statement made to Stansbury Hagar and recorded by him in the story of "The Celestial Bear," *JAF* 13:93-103.

The Mi'kmaq name for the Sun, *Niscaminou,* was first recorded by Father Biard in 1616 (*Jesuit Relations 3:133*). Diereville nearly a century later in his *Relation of the Voyage to Port Royal in Acadia* published in France in 1708 gave *Nickekaminou* as the Mi'kmaq name for the Sun, their creator, and said that it meant "the Very Great." *Nikskam,* modern Mi'kmaq for God, is clearly related to their old name for the sun.

The Passamaquoddy Indians had a tradition that Glooscap shot arrows into an ash tree and through the pierced bark came the Indians (Charles G. Leland;

Algonquin Legends of New England, p. 18). The Mi'kmaq of Cape Breton in one of their tales say that out of the earth of Cape Breton came the mother of the Mi'kmaq (see in this book "How Niscaminou made Glooscap" p. 61. Among the Mi'kmaq in Cape Breton Glooscap is sometimes referred to as "our best grandfather," see Elsie Clews Parsons, "Micmac Folklore," *JAF* 38:85.

In a story told to Champlain by the chief of Tadoussac the Indians were said to have been drawn out of the earth with arrows which the creator had thrust into the ground. (*Works of Samuel De Champlain* 1 :55).

Niscaminou and the Squirrels of Blue Mountain.

This tale of the squirrels of Blue Mountain is based on material in Osgood's *Maritime Provinces* p. 115. In tales of the Passamaquoddy and Penobscot Indians recorded by Dr. Charles Leland: *Algonquin Legends of New England,* p. 29, and by Dr. Frank Speck: "Penobscot Tales and Religious Beliefs," *JAF* 48:49, it was Glooscap who made the squirrels the small and harmless animals they are today. Squirrel's body made smaller, often by squeezing, in this story by looking, is motif A2302.3.

TALES OF THE MOON AND THE STARS

The Sisters Who Married Stars.

This tale of the two girls who married stars is from the two versions of the story in Dr. Rand's *Legends of the Micmacs,* "The Badger and the Star Wives," p. 306, and the "Two Weasels" p. 160. A Cape Breton variant of this story has been recorded by Elsie Clews Parsons: "Micmac Folklore," *JAF* 38:65. Dr. Charles Leland gives a Mi'kmaq and Passamaquoddy version among "The Merry Tales of Lox, the Mischief-Maker": *Algonquin Legends of New England,* pp. 140-207.

The Star Husband theme is a popular one among Indian storytellers. Erminie Wheeler-Voegelin citing Gladys A. Reichard: *Standard Dictionary of Folklore, Mythology, and Legend,* p. 1081, says there are 51 versions of the story of the Star Husbands told by tribes extending from the North Pacific coast to the New England coast. Since 1921, when the Reichard analysis was published, several other versions of the story have been collected and published. The story incorporates, among others, motif A762.1. Stith Thompson: *The Folktale* pp. 345-348, and *Tales of the North American Indians,* pp. 126, 128, Nos. 50, 51, n. 193 gives other types and an analysis of the Star Husband story.

Mooin and the Seven Hunters.

This myth from the *JAF* 13:93-103, was collected by Stansbury Hagar from the Mi'kmaq of Nova Scotia. The only variant to the tale which he heard from Yarmouth to Whycocomagh was an explanation of the red on robin's breast which some of the Indians said was caused when he fell into the fire while the meat was being cooked. The old Mi'kmaq believed that the animals of the earth are descendants of ancestor-animals in the sky, and that their appearance and their habits here on earth reflect the appearance and habits of their ancestors in the sky. The apparent ability of the bear to die and to come back to life in the spring greatly impressed the Mi'kmaq. To be able to do this they believed the bear possessed great magical power and they regarded all bears as sacred animals. The four stars of the constellation Ursa Major seemed to the Mi'kmaq to behave as the bear on the earth.

Father Chretien LeClercq (*New Relation of Gaspesia,* p. 135) heard a fragment of this old tale for he recorded that the Indians of Gaspe knew the Great and Little Bear as *Mouhinnie* and *Mouhinchicle.* The tail of *Mouhinnie* they called the three guards of the North Star — a great canoe in which three Indians are embarked to overtake the bear which they have never been able to catch. The ancient Wabanaki "Song of the Stars," (Leland: *Algonquin Legends of New England,* p. 379), which must have been sung by many of the Mi'kmaq, expresses the old Indian idea of the stars and the three hunters who chase the bear.

> We are the stars which sing,
> We sing with our light;
> We are the birds of fire,
> We fly over the sky.
> Our light is a voice;
> We make a road for spirits,
> For the spirits to pass over.
> Among us are three hunters
> Who chase a bear;
> There never was a time
> When they were not hunting.
> We look down on the mountains.
> This is the Song of the Stars.

The constellation Ursa Major has been the subject of etiological myth and folklore in almost every nation that lives beneath it. Among the North American Indians the story of the bear and the hunters, with definite variations, is known from Coast to Coast, and from North to South. In the Penobscot tale, (Speck:

"Penobscot Tales and Religious Beliefs," *JAF* 48: 19), as the blood from bear's side filled chickadee's dipper it overflowed and fell on the earth below and reddened the leaves of the trees, and the white grease dripping from bear's body became snow upon the earth, and thus came winter.

Moon Chief.

This story was told by Isabelle Googoo Morris to Elsie Clews Parsons in 1923 and is recorded in "Micmac Folklore," *JAF* 38:93-94. The Mi'kmaq, like some other American Indians, (*Standard Dictionary of Folkore, Mythology, and Legend,* 2:744-745), were not consistent with the moon's sex. In this tale the moon is male and in prayers recorded by Father Maillard: *Customs and Manners of the Mickmakes and Maricheets,* pp. 47-48, the moon is female and is addressed as the Sun's wife and as the mother of the Mi'kmaq.

TALES OF THE ORIGIN OF THINGS

How the Loon Became a Sea Bird.

This intriguing tale of the origin of the wild laughter of the loon, so different from the plaintive cry taught the loons by Glooscap in the story "The Call of the Loon", (see page 66 in this book), I heard in the summer of 1961 from Abram Bartlett, a Mi'kmaq Indian of Yarmouth, Nova Scotia. Here is a story showing Negro-Indian exchange of theme and points to Brer Rabbit and the brier patch. To the Negroes and the Indians suffering from long years of oppression tales of the weak outwitting the strong provided a chuckle of laughter as they identified themselves with the victor.

How the Bullfrog Got His Hunched Back.

The story of how the bullfrog got his hunched back is one of many tales about *Kitpooseagunow,* ("The History of Kitpooseagunow," Rand: *Legends of the Micmacs,* pp. 62-80). There are other Mi'kmaq, as well as Passamaquoddy and Penobscot versions of the bullfrog story: Leland: *Algonquin Legends of New England,* pp. 114-119; and Speck: "Penobscot Tales and Religious Beliefs," *JAF* 48:42-43, in which Glooscap kills Chief Bullfrog.

In a Maliseet version (Speck: *JAF* 30:480-482, No.2) the trunk of a tree used by the hero to crush bullfrog became the St. John River; its branches the tributaries of the St. John; its leaves the ponds at the heads of the streams. In the Cape Breton story (Parsons: "Micmac Folklore," *JAF* 38:57-58) old bullfrog demanded the gift of a girl for every bucket of water he gave the Indians.

Kitpooseagunow, which means "one born after his mother's death," was a mighty giant-magician. In Mi'kmaq tales he is second only to the great Glooscap, sharing with him many of the exploits that delight the old storytellers.

Water kept by a monster, sometimes a giant frog, so that mankind cannot us it is motif A1111.

Indian Corn and Tobacco.

This old Mi'kmaq tale embodying the world-wide story-theme of Orpheus seeking a soul in the Land of the Dead was told to Father Chretien LeClercq: *New Relation of Gaspesia,* p. 209. In a story told by John Newell of Pictou Landing, Nova Scotia, (Wallis: *The Micmac Indians of Eastern Canada,* pp. 399-400) a woman and a little girl, lost in the woods, found a patch of corn. They took an ear home, roasted it, and liked it. The woman showed it to her neighbours. It was the first grain they had to eat, and they decided to roast it and save it to make soup with moose meat in the winter. They put the corn around the fire, roasted it, and danced around it in thankfulness for corn.

Quest to the other world for a relative is motif H1252.

The Storm-Maker.

The story of the Storm-Maker is part of "Tumilkoontaoo" (Broken Wing) in Silas T. Rand's *Legends of the Micmacs,* p. 360. The Penobscot and Passamaquoddy Indians have tales of the great StormMaker in which Glooscap was the hero, (Speck: "Penobscot Tales and Religious Beliefs," *JAF* 48:40-41; Leland: *Algonquin Legends of New England,* pp. 111-112). The story of a mighty bird who stirs the winds into motion with his wings is world-wide. Winds caused by flapping of wings is motif A1125, and occurs in Babylonian, Indian, Norse and Icelandic mythology, and in North American Indian (Mi'kmaq, Maliseet, Penobscot, and Passamaquoddy) versions. There is also a Gullah negro story of the Storm-Maker.

The Little People.

This story of the Indian who insulted one of the Little People is from "A Fairy Tale," Rand: *Legends of the Micmacs,* p. 367, an experience which Dr. Rand's informants told him happened to an Indian named Ned Jeddore. In Scandinavian mythology the Night Elves, like the Mi'kmaq' Little People, dwelt in caves and cliffs, and their language, like the Little Peoples', was the echo of solitudes.

The Three Brothers and the Little People.

The three brothers who knew the Little People is retold from "The Fairy," Rand: *Legends of the Micmacs,* p. 431, a story which was told to Dr. Rand by Nancy Jeddore in 1871. The Little People, the diminutive Spirits that dwell in lonely places, in wild forest lands, in fields and streams, are part of the folklore of nearly all the people of the world. In Mi'kmaq, as in the folklore of several Indian tribes, the Little People are tricky and unreliable in their relations with man.

The Indian Who Became a Megumoowesoo.

The Megumoowesoo is an intriguing concept of the spirit of the woodlands. This tale of an Indian who became a Megumoowesoo is from Rand: *Legends of the Micmacs,* p. 94. The description of the *peepoogwen* is from Parsons: "Micmac Folklore," *JAF* 38:63, n 3. The Megumoowesoo has been described by Dr. Frank Speck: "Penobscot Tales and Religious Beliefs," *JAF* 48:16, and by Stansbury Hagar: "Micmac Magic and Medicine," *JAF* IX pp. 170-177, as a little fellow, waist high, and very strong, who lives in the woods and comes when wished for. He wears a single red feather in his hair, and is a master magician. A drawing of a Mikumwess (Passamaquoddy transliteration of Megumoowesoo) scraped on birch bark by Tomah Josephs for Dr. Charles Leland, and used as a frontispiece in *Algonquin Legends of New England,* shows him with his pipe, a small, mischievous, puck-like creature, and wearing a cap which was said to be always a red one.

The Invisible Hunter.

This Cinderella story of the Mi'kmaq, evidently a descendant of an ancient celestial myth, is part of "The Invisible Boy" told to Dr. Rand by Susan Barss in Charlottetown, Prince Edward Island, in the winter of 1848, and recorded in *Legends of the Micmacs,* p. 101. In "The Invisible One," Leland: *Algonquin Legends of New England,* p. 303, the sled string used by the Invisible Hunter was a rainbow; his bow string the Spirit Road, the Milky Way. There is also a Cape Breton version in Parsons: "Micmac Folklore," *JAF* 38:77. Invisibility is a theme of folktales all over the world and is motif 01361.

How Summer Was Brought Back to the Land of the Mi'kmaq.

The tale of how summer was brought back to the Land of the Mi'kmaq is a story collected by Elsie Clews Parsons from Isabelle Googoo Morris, "They Fetch Summer," *JAF* 38:73. In a story recorded by Dr. Charles Leland: *Algonquin Legends of New England,* p. 134, which was collected by Mrs. W. Wallace Brown from Noel Neptune, a Penobscot Indian of Old Town, Maine, Glooscap went into the south land and found summer and brought her to the north and overcame winter.

In Mi'kmaq, as in many other North American Indian Folktales, lady bear is kind and motherly to unhappy or lost Indian children.

TALES OF THE GREAT GLOOSCAP

How Niscaminou Made Glooscap.

The traditions in this story of the creation of Glooscap are from *Folklore of Nova Scotia* by Mary L. Fraser (Sister St. Thomas of the Angels), and from Dr. Frank Speck's "Some Micmac Tales from Cape Breton Island," *JAF* 28:59, and from his book *Beothuk and Micmac,* p. 146. There are several traditions respecting Glooscap's origin among the Indians besides this story of his creation and the tale of Glooscap and his twin brother, Malsum. (See p. 62 in this book). The Mi'kmaq who lived along the Bay of Fundy shores of Nova Scotia said that Glooscap came to them from the east, but they did not have any tales as to how he came into existence. Another Mi'kmaq tradition (Hagar: *JAF* 1 x 173) is that he was the seventh son of one of the first master-magicians, a Megumoowesoo. The Penobscot Indians had no creation or birth traditions for their Gluskabe. To them Gluskabe appeared, and with his coming came a great new way of life for the Indians.

Among the Mi'kmaq Glooscap's old Grandmother, Noogumich, was Mooinaskw, Mrs. Bear; among the Passamaquoddy and Penobscot Indians she was Woodchuck. Hiawatha fans will recognize Nokomis in Noogumich, a term widespread in North American Indian language for Grandmother. The culture hero's grandmother is motif A31. Origin of the culture hero is motif A510.

Glooscap and his Twin Brother Malsum.

The Mi'kmaq traditions of Glooscap and his twin brother Malsum were recorded by Dr. Silas T. Rand: *Legends of the Micmacs,* pp. 339-340, a tale told by Gabriel Thomas of Fredericton, New Brunswick; by Osgood: *Maritime Provinces,* p.41; and by Dr. Charles G Leland: *Algonquin Legends of New England,* pp. 15-16, 106-107, from traditions which were told by a Mi'kmaq Indian to Mr. Edward Jack of Fredericton, New Brunswick. Jack also recorded a Maliseet version of this story in "Maliseet Legends," *JAF* 8:196-197. In the various versions different objects are the instrument of death: a handful of bird's down, a fern root, an owl's feather, the root of a pine tree, a flowering rush, a cattail, a bulrush. An old Mi'kmaq when asked, "Who was Glooscap's mother?" answered, "The female turtle." Among the Algonquians the turtle totem is of the highest rank. Twin culture heroes is motif A515.1.1.

Some traditions claim that from beaver's tattling came the long conflict between Glooscap and the beavers — a conflict that ranged from the inland waters of the Bras d'Or Lakes in Cape Breton to Minas Basin and far up the St. John River and on into Lake Temiscouata.

Glooscap and Mikchikch.

There are two versions of this tale of Mikchikch in Rand: *Legends of the Micmacs,* — one an incident in Nancy Jeddore's story of "Glooscap Deserted by his Comrades," pp. 276-278, the other an incident in "A Wizard Carries off Glooscap's Housekeeper," pp. 289-290, told by Thomas Boonis of Cumberland, Nova Scotia, both of which are part of the tale of the abduction of old Grandmother and Little Marten by the evil wizard Winpe. There are also versions of this story in Osgood's *Maritime Provinces,* p.137, and in Dr. Charles G. Leland's *Algonquin Legends of New England,* pp. 51-58. In the version told by Thomas Boonis, Mikchikch, during the contests in which he takes part after Glooscap had made him a handsome young man, when trying to evade his pursuers in a game of ball, leaps up on his wigwam and is caught on the poles of the chimney hole. Glooscap quietly piles fir boughs on the fire, smudges Mikchikch's coat with the smoke spots still seen on the shell of the turtle, disembowels him with a sharp stick and changes him into a turtle. Creation of turtle is motif A2147.

The First Cedar Tree.

This is part of the story of "Glooscap, Kuhkw, and Coolpujot," Rand: *Legends of the Micmacs,* p. 232. It was told to Dr. Rand by the old Mi'kmaq Stephen Hood in 1869. In a Mi'kmaq tale recorded by Leland: *Algonquin Legends of New England,* p. 94, three Indians went to Glooscap for gifts. One was a tall, vain Indian with his hair dressed high, a turkey's long tail feather stuck in his topknot. He asked to be taller and grander than any other Indian. Glooscap changed him into a tall pine tree, turkey feather and all, which can still be seen waving in the wind. The Mi'kmaq say that the pine trees still murmur in their language, "Oh, I am such a great man! Oh, I am such a great Indian!"

    The departed culture hero grants requests to visitors is motif A575. Requests for immortality punished by transformation into a tree is motif Q338.1.

Glooscap's Footprints.

I was told of Glooscap's footprints in the stone along the shores of Meteghan in Digby County, Nova Scotia, by Julia Pictou, a Mi'kmaq Indian, who, at that time, in 1957, lived in Yarmouth County, Nova Scotia. Glooscap's footprints are also said to be in the rocks at Gaspe Bay, Wallis: *The Micmacs of Eastern Canada,* p.333.

The Call of the Loon.

This Mi'kmaq tradition of the lonely cry of the loons, so different from their wild laughter in the story "How the Loon Became a Sea Bird," (see page 42 in this book), is from Rand: *Legends of the Micmacs,* pp. 288-289, and was one of several stories told to Dr. Rand by Thomas Boonis of Cumberland, Nova Scotia, in 1870. Dr. Charles Leland has a similar story in "How Glooscap became friendly with the Loons, and made them his Messengers," *Algonquin Legends of New England,* pp. 50-51.

The Bird Islands.

This version of the story of the Bird Islands off the east coast of Cape Breton, north of Cape Dauphin was told to Dr. MacEdward Leach in the summer of 1949. According to a version recorded by Dr. Frank G. Speck: *JAF* 28:59, and in *Beothuk and Micmac,* p. 146, the islands are the remains of Glooscap's canoe where he left it after it was broken. Two girls at Plaster Cove seeing the broken canoe laughed at Glooscap. He changed them into rocks, telling them that there they would remain forever. At Wreck Cove he threw down his moose-skin canoe-mat when he jumped ashore, and there to this day is a great patch of bare earth where he left the mat to dry. Still another version of the story is recorded in Mary L. Fraser's *Folklore of Nova Scotia.* Returning from an expedition at sea Glooscap saw on either side of his wigwam two girls who were mighty giants. They taunted him with mocking eyes. Enraged, he gripped the sides of his stone canoe in his giant hands and leaped ashore. As he did so, his canoe broke and he changed the pieces into two islands. Staring at the two girls, he shouted, "Stay where you are forever," and turned them to stone.

How Glooscap Left the Mi'kmaq.

There are many traditions why Glooscap left the Mi'kmaq, how he left, and where he went. The traditions in this story of his departure are from Rand: *Legends of the Micmacs,* pp. xlv, 228, 293; Leland: *Algonquin Legends of New England,* p.67; Osgood: *Maritime Provinces,* p.106.

Many of the Indians say that Glooscap went to the far west or to the other side of the North Pole; some say that he went to a faraway starry place, and others, that he went to the south to the end of the earth. An old Mi'kmaq in Cape Breton, who believed that Glooscap still lives in the North, told Dr. Frank Speck that when Peary reached the North Pole, there was Glooscap sitting on the pole, and they spoke to each other (*JAF* 28:60). The Penobscot Indians say that when Glooscap was ready to leave he told old Grandmother that in the land where he was going he would make many arrows, for a great war might come some day and the Indians would need them. "And I," old Grandmother told him, "will make stores of baked crushed corn for our descendants' food when the great war comes." (Speck: *JAF* 48:47) The culture hero departs is motif A560; the expected return of the culture hero is motif A580.

The Great Chief Ulgimoo.

The Mi'kmaq had many tales of their long conflict with the Mohawks. This tale of the warrior-chief Ulgimoo is part of the "History of the Celebrated Chief, Ulgimoo," *Legends of the Micmacs,* pp. 294-297, as told to Dr. Rand by the Mi'kmaq, Thomas Boonis, of Cumberland, Nova Scotia. The soul enters a body and animates it is motif E726.

Wokun.

The story of the knife in Bloody Creek, Shelburne County, Nova Scotia, was told to me by the Mi'kmaq Indian, the late James Michael of Barrington, Nova Scotia, who heard it as a boy from his Indian people. This story was selected by Maria Leach from my collection of Mi'kmaq tales, and was included in her book *The Rainbow Book of American Folk Tales and Legends,* pp. 230-231.

Magua of Refugee Cove.

This story I heard from Mrs. Yvonne Lunn of Advocate, Nova Scotia, in the summer of 1961. It was told as she had heard it from the people of Advocate as they remembered the tale told by the old Mi'kmaq. Two stories of a wife deserted are recorded by Speck: "Penobscot Tales and Religious Beliefs," *JAF* 48:86-87. In each tale the wife is left on an island, and when she is found, her husband is killed by her relatives.

Memajoookun.

This story from "The Hidden Life," *Legends of the Micmacs,* p. 245, was recorded by Dr. Rand in bare outline as he recalled it several days after he heard it from the Mi'kmaq Stephen Hood. The story is of particular interest for its use of the external soul (E710) in restoring life to a dismembered corpse, motif E422.1.10. A hidden soul is motif E712.

BIBLIOGRAPHY

Akins, Thomas B: *Selections from the Public Documents of the Province of Nova Scotia,* Charles Annand, Halifax, 1869.

Anderson, William P: *Micmac Place-Names,* Surveyor General's Office, Ottawa, 1919.

Campbell, Duncan: *Nova Scotia, in its Historical, Mercantile, and Industrial Relations,* John Lovell, Montreal, 1873.

Champlain, Samuel de: *The Works of Samuel de Champlain,* Vol. 1., Edited by H. P. Biggar, The Champlain Society, Toronto, 1922.

Chard, Elizabeth Hutton: "Truckhouse Trading," *Journal of Education,* Vol. 15, No. 3, pp. 20-24, Halifax, Nova Scotia, February, 1966.

Cormack, W. E: *A Journey Across the Island of Newfoundland in 1822,* Edited by F. A. Brunton, Longmans, Green & Co., Ltd., New York and London, 1928.

Denys, Nicolas: *The Description and Natural History of the Coasts of North America (Acadia),* Translated and edited by William F. Ganong, The Champlain Society, Toronto, 1908.

Diereville, le Sieur de: *Relation of the Voyage to Port Royal in Acadia or New France,* English translation by Mrs. Clarence Webster, edited by John Clarence, Webster, The Champlain Society, Toronto, 1933. 1st Ed., 1708.

Erskine, J. S: "Their Crowded Hour: The Micmac Cycle," *Dalhousie Review,* Vol. 38, No.4, pp. 443-452, Winter, 1959.

—: "Nova Scotia Prehistory," *Dalhousie Review,* Vol. 44, No.1, pp. 16-27, Spring, 1964.

—: "Before Jacques Cartier," *Journal of Education,* Series 5, Vol. 9, No.2, pp. 65-70, Halifax, Nova Scotia, June, 1960.

—: *Micmac Notes, 1960, Occasional Papers, No.1, Archaeological Series No.1,* Nova Scotia Museum, Halifax, Nova Scotia, February, 1961.

Fraser, Mary L: *Folklore of Nova Scotia,* Sydney, Nova Scotia. Publisher and date of publication not given.

Ganong, W. F: "A Monograph of the Place-Nomenclature of the Province of New Brunswick," *Transactions Royal Society of Canada,* 1896.

Hagar, Stansbury: "The Celestial Bear," *Journal of American Folklore,* 13:93-103, (1900).

—: "Micmac Magic and Medicine," *Journal of American Folklore,* 9:170-177, (1896).

Hodge, Frederick Webb: "Micmac," *Handbook of American Indians North of Mexico,* 1:858-859, Bureau of American Ethnology, Bulletin 30, Government Printing Office, Washington, D.C., 1907.

Hoffman, Bernard G: "Souriquois, Etchemin, and Kwedech — A Lost Chapter in American Ethnography," *Ethohistory,* Vol. 2, No.1., pp. 65-87, Winter, 1955

Hollingsworth, S: *The Present State of Nova Scotia,* Edinburgh, 1787.

Homen, Diego: *Map, Northeast part of North America,* 1558.

Hutton, Elizabeth Ann: "Indian Affairs in Nova Scotia, 1760-1834," *Collections Nova Scotia Historical Society,* 34:33-54, (1963).

Jack, Edward: Summary of an article in the Fredericton Trade Review, December 15, 1887, on legends of Glooscap, *Journal of American Folklore,* 1:85, (1888).

—: "Maliseet Legends," *Journal of American Folklore,* 8:193-208, (1895). Jefferys, C. W: *The Picture Gallery of Canadian History, 1763 to 1830,* Vol. 2, p. 215, Ryerson Press, Toronto, 1953, Fourth Printing.

Jenness, Diamond: *The Indians of Canada,* Bulletin 65, National Museum of Canada, Ottawa, 1932.

Jesuit Relations and Allied Documents, Vols. 1, 2, 3, 4, 7, 8, Edited by Reuben Gold Thwaites, The Burrows Brothers Company, Cleveland, Ohio, 1896.

Knox, John: *An Historical Journal of the Campaigns in North America for the Years 1757, 1758, 1759 and 1760,* edited by Arthur G. Doughty, The Champlain Society, Toronto, 1914.

Leach, Maria: *Rainbow Book of American Folk Tales and Legends,* World Publishing Company, Cleveland and New York, 1958.

—: *God Had a Dog,* Rutgers University Press, New Brunswick, New Jersey, 1961.

Leach, Maria and Jerome Fried: *Standard Dictionary of Folklore, Mythology, and Legend,* 2 vols., Funk and Wagnalls Company, New York, 1949-1950.

LeClercq, Chretien: *New Relation of Gaspesia,* Translated and edited by William F. Ganong, The Champlain Society, Toronto, 1910.

Leland, Charles G: *Algonquin Legends of New England, or Myths and Folk Lore of the Micmacs, Passamaquoddy, and Penobscot Tribes,* The Riverside Press, Cambridge, 1884.

Lescarbot, Marc: *The History of New France,* 3 vols., English translation by W. L. Grant, The Champlain Society, Toronto, 1914.

Maillard, l'Abbé (Antoine Simon): *An Account of the Customs and Manners of the Mickmakis and Maricheets, Savage Nations, Now Dependent on the Government of Cape Breton,* London, 1758.

Michelson, Truman: "Micmac Tales," *Journal American Folklore,* 38:33-54, (1925).

Murdock, Beamish: *A History of Nova Scotia,* 3 vols., James Barnes, Printer and Publisher, Halifax, 1865-1867.

Osgood: *Maritime Provinces,* 1875. Publisher not given.

Parsons, Elsie Clews: "Micmac Folklore," *Journal of American Folklore,* 38:55-133, (1925).

—: "Micmac Notes," *Journal of American Folklore,* 39:460-485, (1926), Patterson, George: "The Beothuks or Red Indians of Newfoundland," *Trans. Royal Society of Canada,* Section 11, 1891.

—: *A History of the County of Pictou, Nova Scotia,* Gazette Printing House, Montreal, 1877.

Public Archives of Nova Scotia, *Manuscript Documents of Nova Scotia,* Vol. 228, Docs. 102,103,104,105,106,108.

Rand, Silas T: *Dictionary of the Language of the Micmac Indians,* Nova Scotia Printing Company, Halifax, 1888.

—: *Micmac Dictionary,* Edited by J. S. Clark, Patriot Publishing Company, Charlottetown, Prince Edward Island, 1902.

—: *Micmac Place-Names,* Edited by William P. Anderson, Surveyor General's Office, Ottawa, 1919.

—: *Legends of the Micmacs,* Longmans, Green, and Co., New York, 1894.

—: *A First Reading Book in the Micmac Language,* Nova Scotia Printing Company, Halifax, 1875.

—: *Reports Micmac Missionary Society,* Halifax, 1859, 1882.

Reade, John: "Some Wabanki Songs," *Trans. Royal Society of Canada,* Section 11, pp.1-8, 1887.

—: "Aboriginal American Poetry," *Trans. Royal Society of Canada,* Section 11, pp. 9-34, 1887.

Roth, D. Luther: *Acadia and the Acadians,* Lutheran Publication Society, Philadelphia, 1890.

Speck, Frank G: *Beothuk and Micmac,* Haye Foundation, New York, 1922.

—: "Some Micmac Tales From Cape Breton Island," *Journal of American Folklore,*
28:59-69, (1915).

—: "Penobscot Tales and Religious Beliefs," *Journal of American Folklore,*
48:1-107, (1935).

Smith, Harlan I. and W. J. Wintemberg: *Some Shell-Heaps in Nova Scotia,* Bulletin 47,
National Museum of Canada, Ottawa, 1929.

Smith, Titus: *Diary of Titus Smith,* Manuscript Document, Vol. 380, Public
Archives of Nova Scotia.

Stoddard, Natalie B: "Indian Tools of Nova Scotia," *Journal of Education,* vol. 15,
No.2, pp. 24-31, Halifax, Nova Scotia, December, 1965.

—: "Micmac Foods," *Journal of Education,* vol. 15, No. 3, pp. 31-37, Halifax, Nova
Scotia, February, 1966.

Swanton, John R: *The Indian Tribes of North America,* Smithsonian Institution
Bureau of American Ethnology, Bulletin 145, Government Printing Office,
Washington, 1953.

Thompson, Stith: *Tales of the North American Indians,* Harvard University Press,
Cambridge, Mass., 1929.

—: *The Folktale,* Dryden Press, New York, 1946.

—: *Motif-Index of Folk Literature,* 2nd ed., 6 vols., Indiana University Press,
Bloomington, 1955-1958.

Wallis, Wilson D. and Ruth Sawtell Wallis: *The Micmac Indians of Eastern Canada,*
University of Minnesota Press, Minneapolis.

Webster, J. Clarence: *An Historical Guide to New Brunswick,* New Brunswick
Government Bureau, 1944.

Wheeler-Voegelin, Erminie: article Star Husband, Star Boy, *Standard Dictionary of
Folklore, Mythology, and Legend,* p. 1081.